CHOCOLATE

Dom Ramsey

CONTENTS

CHOCOLATE OBSESSIVE

This book explores the world of chocolate in detail, helping you to **understand** how it transforms from the cacao tree to the bar, and to **explore** the key cacao-growing regions in the world. Discover how to **choose** the best-quality varieties, appreciating the flavours every time you **taste**. Learn how to **create** your own chocolate at home, using cocoa beans, sugar, and some simple equipment. Feel inspired to make and **enjoy** a remarkable selection of recipes from the world's finest chocolatiers, pastry chefs, and chocolate experts.

DISCOVER THE PEOPLE AND TRADITIONS BEHIND CHOCOLATE

When I started my journey with chocolate in 2006, I knew very little about the dark and mysterious food. After discovering hand-made fresh truffles and single-origin hand-crafted bars, I was hooked. It wasn't only tasting the chocolate, it was also meeting the people behind it that opened my eyes to the wonderful world of chocolate – innovative chocolatiers, dedicated and passionate bean-to-bar chocolate makers, and the people who made it all possible, the often-exploited cocoa farmers. These people inspired me to open my own bean-to-bar company, Damson Chocolate, with a very simple aim – to produce the best chocolate I can.

The world of chocolate is fascinating and absorbing. I hope this book inspires you to delve deeper into the subject, just as my chocolate heroes inspired me.

DOM RAMSEY

Chocolate contributors

These international pastry chefs, chocolatiers, mixologists, and food writers have joined forces to create the sweet and savoury chocolate recipes in this book.

Bruno Breillet
Bruno is the award-winning Head Pastry Chef and co-owner of Bruno's Bakes and Coffee in Kent, UK. Bruno grew up in Lyon, France, and specializes in American–French delights. He is also an event creator, caterer, and recipe developer.

Caroline Bretherton
Cookery writer Caroline is the author of five cookery books, including DK's bestselling *Step-by-Step Baking*. She has a passion for fresh ingredients and contemporary recipes, particularly of the sweet variety. She now works from her home in North Carolina, USA.

Jesse Carr
Growing up in Virginia, USA, Jesse made drinks for his grandparents. The mixologist refined his trade in the saloons of New York, including Maison Premiere. Jesse lives in New Orleans and is bar director of La Petite Grocery and Balise.

Micah Carr-Hill
Micah is a food writer, food scientist, product developer, and taste consultant. He has worked on Green & Black's Chocolate and Pump Street Bakery Chocolate.

Lisabeth Flanagan
Lisabeth is a chocolatier and chocolate reviewer based on Canada's Manitoulin Island. She owns Ultimately Chocolate, a gourmet dessert-making business, and writes about chocolate weekly on *The Ultimate Chocolate Blog*.

Charlotte Flower
A chocolatier based in rural Perthshire, Scotland, Charlotte makes truffles and chocolates that bring together wild flavours from the stunning surrounding landscape with chocolate from around the world.

Bryan Graham
Bryan is the founder of the bean-to-bar chocolate company Fruition Chocolate Works and Confectionery, based in the Catskill Mountains in New York State. Before becoming a chocolate maker, Bryan worked as a pastry chef in Woodstock, New York.

Christian Hümbs
Christian is a trained chef and pâtissier, who has worked as a pastry chef in several renowned and Michelin-starred restaurants in Germany. Christian is the author of DK's *Bake to Impress*.

Edd Kimber
Edd is a baker, food writer, and TV personality based in the UK. He is the author of three cookbooks, and writer of the award-winning blog *The Boy Who Bakes*.

William (Bill) McCarrick
Bill is Pastry Chef Instructor at the Culinary Institute of America in New York, USA. He trained in Europe and became an award-winning pastry chef in Asia, before moving to London to oversee all chocolate and pastry at Harrods. In 2005, he founded Hans Sloane Chocolate in Surrey, UK.

Maricel E. Presilla
A founder of the International Chocolate Awards, Maricel is an award-winning chef and cookery writer specializing in the foods of Latin America and Spain. She is also President of Gran Cacao Company, a chocolate research company that specializes in premium cacao beans from Latin America.

Paul A. Young
Paul is an award-winning chocolatier, chocolate-shop owner, and cookery writer based in London, UK. Paul worked as Head Pastry Chef for Marco Pierre White at Quo Vadis and Criterion, before specializing in chocolate. In 2014, Paul was named Outstanding British Chocolatier by the International Chocolate Awards.

INTRODUCTION

For more than 4,000 years, we've been enjoying chocolate in various forms. Trace chocolate's incredible journey around the world and its transformation into the indulgence we love today.

THE CHOCOLATE REVOLUTION

Chocolate was consumed as a bitter, spiced drink for thousands of years until the mid-1800s, when the chocolate bar took the world by storm. Today, another chocolate revolution is taking shape – an international craft chocolate movement is generating fine-quality chocolate using artisan techniques and fresh ingredients.

CHOCOLATE LIBRARY
There is now an increasing number of international chocolate makers creating fine-flavour chocolate, from bean to bar.

A FRESH APPROACH

J.S. Fry & Sons introduced the world's first chocolate bar in the mid-19th century, and confectionery companies have been fighting for our custom ever since. With new formats and flavours, manufacturers are constantly striving to find something new to grab our attention.

Large manufacturers face a big challenge – to make enough chocolate to satisfy the world's ever-growing demands. This task, coupled with an increasing need to minimize costs, means that manufacturers seek out high-yielding cacao varieties at the lowest possible price. Every year, millions of tonnes of this cheap cocoa finds its way into the confectionery we know and love. However, many large manufacturers have overlooked one all-important aspect: the quality of the cocoa itself.

The craft chocolate movement is gaining momentum, and brings a renewed emphasis on the quality, flavour, and sustainability of cocoa beans. Craft chocolate makers from around the world are promoting a new respect for the whole process of making chocolate – from the cacao tree to the chocolate bar.

FROM TREE TO BAR
Craft chocolate makers have an extreme commitment to quality. They produce carefully crafted chocolate from scratch to get the best possible flavour from every cocoa bean.

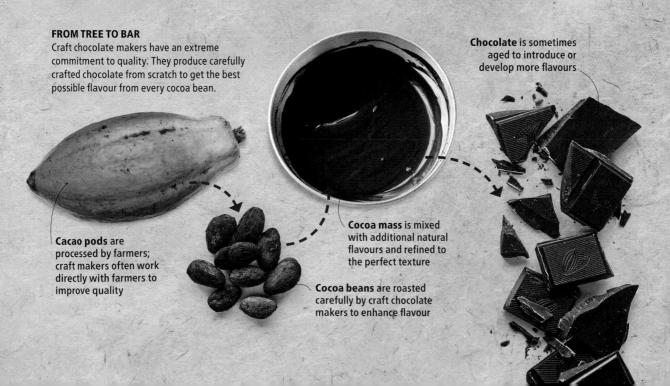

Chocolate is sometimes aged to introduce or develop more flavours

Cocoa mass is mixed with additional natural flavours and refined to the perfect texture

Cacao pods are processed by farmers; craft makers often work directly with farmers to improve quality

Cocoa beans are roasted carefully by craft chocolate makers to enhance flavour

NEW CHOC ON THE BLOCK

Craft makers and artisan chocolatiers have been at the heart of the worldwide chocolate revolution. Embracing quality, sustainability, and ethics, these pioneers have introduced new international trends to the chocolate industry.

Fairtrade and organic

Many makers have pushed for improvements in the traceability and sustainability of chocolate. There's a growing awareness of the issues of poverty and child labour in the industry, and this has increased the demand for chocolate that is produced fairly and sustainably. An increasing number of brands work with the Fairtrade Foundation, and craft chocolate makers in particular often work directly with farmers, paying a premium for fine-flavour beans and helping to improve quality and conditions.

Bean to bar

In the mid-1990s, a few creative chocolate lovers from the US were tired of the chocolate on the market and decided to make good-quality chocolate from scratch. They became the first of a new wave of craft bean-to-bar makers, undertaking the entire chocolate-making process themselves, from cocoa beans to finished bars.

Sourcing the best ingredients they could find and building chocolate-making machinery from scratch, they introduced a new kind of chocolate to consumers. Craft chocolate makers increased in number, and today there are more than 300 of them in the US alone.

At first, the rest of the world was a little slow to catch on, but as the cost of machinery started to fall, more and more bean-to-bar makers appeared around the world – each with their own unique style and approach to chocolate-making, and a passion for quality and flavour.

Tree to bar

For hundreds of years, cocoa was grown and processed in equatorial regions, but then transformed into chocolate in other parts of the world. Within the last two decades, there has been an exciting increase in the number of chocolate factories in cacao-growing countries, in part because there is more monetary value in selling chocolate bars than growing cacao. This new kind of chocolate maker creates chocolate from the tree to the bar, and is helping to transform economies in some of the poorest parts of the world.

Artisan chocolates

Alongside the revolution in chocolate-making, new methods for making filled chocolates, pralines, and truffles are transforming the traditional box of chocolates. Artisan chocolatiers are switching to fresh ingredients and single-origin chocolate, seeking out the perfect match of chocolate and filling. These "fresh chocolates" are produced without preservatives, so have a short shelf life. Adventurous chocolatiers play with a wide array of flavours — from simple ganaches and fruit caramels to exotic spices and traditionally savoury ingredients, such as herbs, cheeses, or even bacon.

Single origin

Inspired by success in the wine and coffee industries, chocolate makers have started to source cocoa from unusual locations to produce single-origin chocolate bars.

Most cocoa used in confectionery chocolate comes from West Africa, where high-yield, low-flavour varieties dominate. Craft chocolate makers have focused on varieties with more complex and unique flavours from Central America, The Caribbean, and parts of Asia.

CHOCOLATE ORIGINS

The peoples of the Americas have been enjoying chocolate for at least 3,500 years. Chocolate was first consumed in liquid form during religious ceremonies, and became one of the most highly valued commodities in ancient Mesoamerica. It is thought that communities traded the beans for brightly coloured feathers, precious stones, and cloth.

COCOA IN THE ANCIENT WORLD

Long before the arrival of the Spanish *conquistadores* in the 16th century, chocolate had a complex history spanning ancient Mesoamerica. The earliest communities of Central America drank cocoa, and the custom continued for thousands of years.

MANY OF THE ANCIENT EMPIRES REVERED COCOA

Mesoamerica covered an area from present-day central Mexico to northern Costa Rica. The region was ruled by a series of powerful empires, including the Olmecs, Mayans, and Aztecs, all of whom revered cocoa. First the cacao pulp, and later cocoa beans, were ground into a liquid and consumed as a thick drink (see pp16–17), usually by the ruling elite.

ARCHAEOLOGICAL DISCOVERIES

Cacao is the only plant that grew in ancient Mesoamerica containing both of the chemicals caffeine and theobromine (see right). Researchers analyzing pieces of pottery are able to determine which pots once contained cocoa, based on the presence of these chemicals. The earliest-known evidence of cacao consumption was found at Paso de la Amada, near Soconusco in Mexico.

MOKAYA POTTERY
In the early 2000s, a large quantity of pottery was uncovered at Paso de la Amada in present-day Mexico. The area was once a village inhabited by the Mokaya, who were early settlers in the region.

Pottery shards were analyzed by researchers in order to date the pots and find out what they contained

Theobromine molecule

Caffeine molecule

Theobromine and caffeine molecules – indicating the presence of cacao – were found on a pottery shard dating from 1900–1500 BCE

Chaco Canyon

CENTRAL AMERICA

NAMING CACAO
The word "cacao" is used to this day to refer to the cacao tree and its pods and beans. The word is likely to have its roots in the ancient Mayan term for cacao, "kakaw". In 1753, the famous Swedish botanist Carolus Linnaeus gave the tree its scientific name: *Theobroma cacao*, or "food-of-the-gods cacao". In the chocolate industry today, cacao and the anglicized "cocoa" are used interchangeably; this book uses *cacao* to refer to the tree, pods, and beans prior to fermentation, and then *cocoa* thereafter.

THE CARIBBEAN

El Manatí

Río Azul

Mesoamerica stretched from central Mexico to northern Costa Rica; experts believe that chocolate was consumed here in 1900 BCE

Paso de la Amada

Maracaibo

The Andes

EARLY TRAVELS
Most experts believe that the cacao tree originated in the the Amazon basin and that Central American cacao descended from trees in the foothills of the Andes and from Maracaibo in Venezuela. As ancient peoples traded with one another, cacao gradually made its way northwards.

The Mokaya people living in Paso de la Amada were consuming cocoa in 1900 BCE, and the Olmecs of El Manatí were drinking cocoa about 200 years later. Mayans living near the Río Azul in the 5th century cooked foods flavoured with cocoa beans. By 1100, cocoa had travelled as far north as the Chaco Canyon in present-day New Mexico. The Aztecs (1345–1521) were fervent cocoa-drinkers, and passed the custom on to the Spanish.

SOUTH AMERICA

THE CACAO TREE ORIGINATED IN THE RAINFORESTS OF THE AMAZON BASIN

DRINKING CHOCOLATE

For thousands of years, chocolate was consumed as a drink, but it bore almost no resemblance to the sweet hot chocolate we drink today. The drink was made from ground cocoa beans, water, and cornmeal, and flavoured with vanilla, chillies, and fragrant flowers.

SACRED CACAO

Of all the great, cocoa-drinking civilizations of Central America, most is known about the Aztecs, who were in power between 1345 and 1521 CE. The Aztecs, along with the Mokaya, Olmecs, and Mayans, believed that cocoa was a divine food from the gods, and used it in religious ceremonies and important celebrations. The beans were also used as currency across later empires – colonized territories had to pay annual tributes in cocoa beans.

ACHIOTE SEEDS
Mayans often coloured their cocoa red using a paste made from achiote (or annatto) seeds. This process made the cocoa look like the blood of sacrificial victims, increasing its symbolic power.

3

2

1

CACAO HARVESTING
Cacao pods were harvested from trees growing locally. The imperial capital of Tenochtitlan (present-day Mexico City) was home to numerous *cacahuateros* (cocoa merchants) selling different grades of beans.

ROASTING OVER FIRE
Once removed from their pods, the beans were roasted over wood fires to bring out natural flavours. The beans are likely to have been dry-roasted in a flat clay dish known as a "comal".

GRINDING IN A METATE
The roasted beans were ground to a thick paste using a metate. A metate consists of an indented, solid stone base to contain the cocoa and a hand-held stone to grind with – before mechanization, it was the most commonly used cocoa-grinding equipment.

DRINKING THE PULP

Some of the earliest cocoa drinks may have been made from the sweet, juicy pulp surrounding the beans in the cacao pod. Archaeological findings in present-day Honduras suggest that these drinks were not flavoured or thickened, unlike those made from cocoa beans. The pulp is likely to have been fermented before being drunk, in order to turn it into an alcholic liquid. Some communities in Central America make alcoholic beverages from cacao pulp to this day.

IN ANCIENT EMPIRES, COCOA BEANS WERE USED AS CURRENCY

4

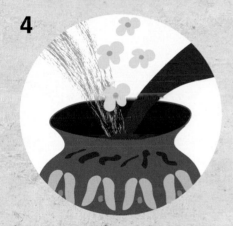

ADDING WATER AND SPICES
Cornmeal or other thickeners were added to the cocoa, along with hot or cold water. The Aztecs called cocoa "xocoatl", or "bitter water", which is probably the origin of the European word "chocolate". The mixture was flavoured with vanilla, chillies, spices, or flowers, and sometimes sweetened with honey or plant sap.

5

POURING
The best-quality cocoa drinks had a thick froth on top; this was formed by repeatedly pouring the cocoa back and forth between earthenware containers. These containers were often highly decorated, to emphasize the ceremonial value of their contents.

6

DRINKING
By the Aztec period, cocoa-drinking had become synonymous with status. It was usually drunk by powerful leaders, warriors, and merchants, often in religious ceremonies or for significant celebrations.

CACAO ON THE MOVE

The journey of cacao from Mesoamerica to other areas of the world is due largely to Europeans, who conquered much of the region and introduced the crop to their colonies across the world.

In the 16th century, the Spanish were the first to introduce cacao to new regions of the Caribbean and Central America, and soon the French followed suit. In the 17th century, the Spanish expanded into other colonies in Central America and used African slave labour to manage the harvests.

Before long, European nations were planting cacao in colonies around the world. The British took it to Ceylon (now Sri Lanka) and India, the Dutch introduced it into Indonesia, while the Spanish spread it further across South America. The Portuguese introduced cacao to Africa in the early 19th century. Beginning with São Tomé, the crop spread quickly, first to the neighbouring island of Fernando Pó (now Bioko), then to mainland Gold Coast (now Ghana).

Largely due to this colonial movement, cacao can now be found growing almost anywhere that conditions allow (see pp26–27).

THE JOURNEY OF CACAO TRADE
This map shows how European influences between 1500 and 1800 encouraged the spread of cacao cultivation from South America to other colonies across the world.

1500s

The Spanish and Portuguese meet increasing demand for chocolate by introducing the crop to their colonies.

• Spain to Trinidad and Tobago, Honduras, Cuba, Venezuela, and Colombia.

• Portugal to Brazil.

1600s

The French saw promise in the crop and introduced cacao to their colonies in the Caribbean. The Spanish trial cacao in Asia.

• France to Dominican Republic and Grenada.

• Spain to the Philippines, Indonesia, and Peru.

Dominican Republic
Cuba
St Lucia
Martinique
Grenada
Honduras
Trinidad and Tobago
Colombia
Venezuela
Peru
Brazil

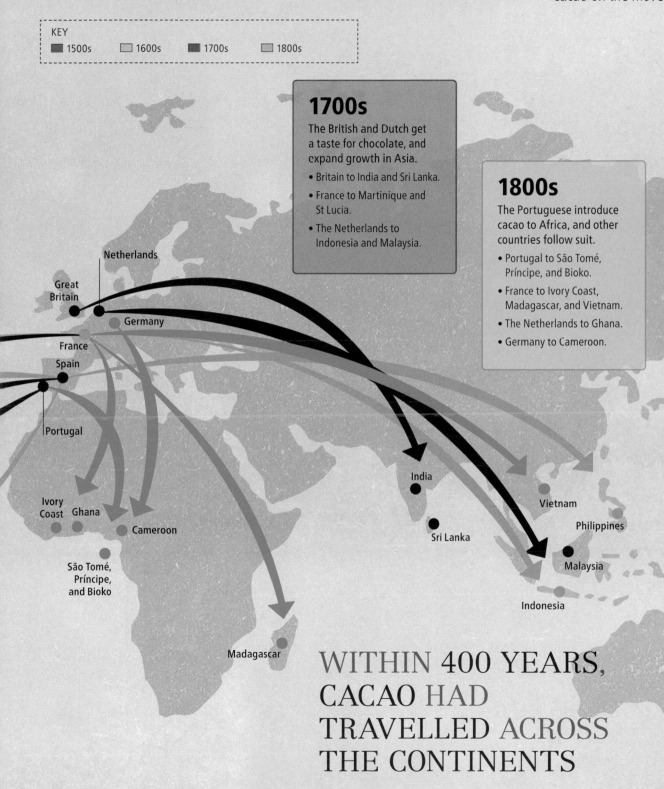

KEY
■ 1500s   □ 1600s   ■ 1700s   □ 1800s

1700s

The British and Dutch get a taste for chocolate, and expand growth in Asia.

- Britain to India and Sri Lanka.
- France to Martinique and St Lucia.
- The Netherlands to Indonesia and Malaysia.

1800s

The Portuguese introduce cacao to Africa, and other countries follow suit.

- Portugal to São Tomé, Príncipe, and Bioko.
- France to Ivory Coast, Madagascar, and Vietnam.
- The Netherlands to Ghana.
- Germany to Cameroon.

WITHIN 400 YEARS, CACAO HAD TRAVELLED ACROSS THE CONTINENTS

CHOCOLATE TRANSFORMED

Chocolate was introduced to Europe in the 16th century by Spanish explorers. First consumed as a bitter spiced drink, chocolate quickly became popular with royalty and the upper classes. It took another 300 years before it became the chocolate bars and confections we enjoy today.

CHOCOLATE IN EUROPE

In around 1590, the Spanish returned home from the conquest of the Aztec empire, bringing cocoa beans with them. They introduced the bitter, spiced cacao drink to Spain, and by the 17th century the drink was popular throughout the country, served hot and sweetened with sugar cane.

Initially a preserve of royalty and the upper classes, the drink gradually became widely available, and popularity spread across Europe. The first recorded appearance in England was in 1657, when a newspaper recommended an "excellent West India drink called chocolate". In 1659, the first chocolatier in France, David Chaillou, prepared biscuits and cakes made with chocolate. By the turn of the 18th century, rowdy chocolate houses were a fixture of London's high society, known as places to gamble, argue politics, and plot mischief.

THE FIRST CHOCOLATE BAR

By the early 1800s, chocolate had become more widely available to the general public, but was still largely consumed as a drink and limited to special occasions. In 1828, a Dutch chemist called Casparus van Houten Senior patented an inexpensive method for pressing the fat from roasted cocoa beans. Van Houten's machine – a hydraulic press – reduced the cocoa butter content in the beans to create a "cake" that could be pulverized into cocoa powder.

1550–1600

In around 1590, the conquistador Hernán Cortés brings chocolate to Spain, and the popularity of the drink spreads throughout Spain, initially with royalty and the upper classes.

1600–1650

In 1606, the Italian trader Francesco Carletti – inspired by travels to the West Indies and Spain – introduces the chocolate drink to Italy. From Italy and Spain, chocolate is introduced to Germany, Austria, Switzerland, France, Belgium, and the Netherlands.

1650–1700

Chocolate has its first recorded appearance in England in 1657. In around 1689, the "chocolate kitchens" were first built at Hampton Court Palace for Queen Mary II. Chocolate is still largely a privilege of the rich in Europe.

In England in 1847, J.S. Fry & Sons produced the world's first moulded chocolate bars. These bars were made from cocoa powder, sugar, and cocoa butter, and would seem very coarse and bitter by modern standards, but proved an instant hit.

TECHNOLOGICAL ADVANCES

The first commercial milk chocolate wasn't created until 1875, almost 30 years after the first chocolate bar.

Swiss chocolate maker Daniel Peter was working with the Swiss confectioner Henri Nestlé and discovered a method of dehydrating milk to remove water. This was key, as moisture is a natural enemy of chocolate, causing it to seize and become unworkable. Even a small trace can lead to mildew forming – a problem which had beset previous attempts to make milk chocolate.

The chocolate-making process was also improved by a method called "conching". Developed by the Swiss inventor Rodolphe Lindt in 1879, the process involves prolonged stirring to improve the flavour of chocolate. Lindt was also one of the first to mix additional cocoa butter through chocolate for a smooth texture – a defining characteristic of Swiss chocolate.

TRUFFLES AND PRALINES

Legend has it that in the early 1900s, an apprentice of the French chef Auguste Escoffier was the first to mix chocolate and cream to create ganache. The story goes that he poured hot cream over a bowl of chocolate by mistake, finding that the mixture was easy to shape into little truffles.

Despite this popular myth, it is likely that ganache was first made in the late 19th century. Whatever its origins, ganache helped chocolatiers to combine other flavours with chocolate, and the fashion for truffles spread across France, Belgium, and the rest of Europe.

CHOCOLATE FACTORY, 1909
Factory workers wrap bars by hand. By the early 20th century, the chocolate industry was booming throughout Europe and the US.

1700–1800

The English state commissioner John Hannon introduces chocolate to the US. Chocolate houses become a fixture of London's high society. In the major cities of Italy, *cioccolatieri* (chocolate shops) are thriving.

1800–1850

Chocolate becomes widely available to the European public. In 1828, the Dutch chemist Casparus van Houten Senior patents the hydraulic press, which is used to turn cocoa nibs into a powder known as "Dutch cocoa".

1850–1900

In England in 1847, J.S. Fry & Sons produce the first moulded dark chocolate bars. In 1875, Swiss chocolate maker Daniel Peter creates milk chocolate. In Switzerland in 1879, Rodolphe Lindt creates the "conching" process.

UNDERSTAND

How is chocolate made? Cocoa begins life as a bean, growing inside pods on the cacao tree. Discover how farmers harvest and process the beans, and how makers transform them into chocolate.

FROM CACAO TREE TO CHOCOLATE BAR

Chocolate is made from the fruit of *Theobroma cacao*, otherwise known as the cacao tree. Cacao must undergo a series of transformations before it becomes recognizable as chocolate – the journey from humid equatorial plantation to beautifully packaged bar has many steps along the way.

STAGE ONE

The first stage is completed by farmers and labourers, on plantations located in the equatorial belt.

1

HARVESTING
When farmers judge the cacao to be ripe, they harvest the pods using a machete, then break the pods open and remove the beans and pulp from inside.

Each pod contains 25–50 cacao beans, surrounded in juicy pulp

2

FERMENTING
Farmers ferment piles of beans in boxes for 5–7 days. The piles are turned every few days to introduce air and ensure even fermentation.

Chemical changes halt germination and transform the bean flavour

3

Some farmers "tramp" the beans as they dry – shuffling through the piles to ensure even drying

DRYING
Farmers lay out the beans in the sun to dry for a week or so, turning them regularly to ensure even drying.

4

TRANSPORTING
Farmers pack the dried beans into breathable burlap sacks and transport them to warehouses or directly to a chocolate maker.

STAGE TWO

Processed cocoa beans are transported to chocolate makers all over the globe, who transform the beans into chocolate.

5

SORTING

Makers remove debris such as twigs, sticks, and broken or mouldy beans.

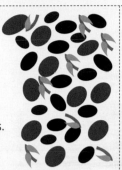

6

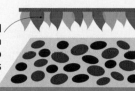

Conventional ovens can be used to roast beans

ROASTING

Makers roast the beans to develop flavour, kill bacteria, and loosen shells.

7

Papery outer shells begin to separate from the nibs inside

BREAKING

After cooling, makers crush the beans into pieces called nibs.

8

WINNOWING

The light outer shells of the beans are blown away with jets of air, leaving just the cocoa nibs behind.

9

GRINDING AND REFINING

Makers grind the nibs into a thick paste known as "cocoa liquor".

Friction melts and releases the cocoa butter inside the nibs

10

ADDING INGREDIENTS

Makers add sugar and cocoa butter to the cocoa liquor. Milk solids or other powdered flavours can also be added.

11

Specialized grinders are commonly used for grinding and conching

CONCHING

Makers move and aerate the molten chocolate, sometimes for several days.

12

SETTING AND AGEING

Makers pour the chocolate into large containers to cool. Some age the solid blocks of chocolate for several weeks to develop flavour even further.

13

TEMPERING

The chocolate is heated, cooled, and reheated to precise temperatures to achieve the perfect crystal structure.

14

MOULDING AND PACKING

The chocolate is now ready to use, and is poured into moulds to make bars or filled chocolates.

THEOBROMA CACAO

The cacao tree, *Theobroma cacao*, originates in the Americas, but can now be found growing on five continents. Cacao grows in hot and humid regions close to the equator, and requires specific conditions in order to thrive and produce perfect fruit.

A GLOBAL CROP

Cacao originated in Central America and the Amazon basin. In the 16th century, Europeans first introduced cacao to their colonies in order to feed a growing worldwide appetite for chocolate.

Today, you can find cacao trees across the world. The hot and humid environments within 20 degrees north or south of the equator provide the ideal growing conditions for cacao, which is usually grown in small plantations in the shade of taller trees, often in or near rainforested areas.

Towards the outer edges of the equatorial belt, it becomes more difficult to produce a sustainable crop; outside of the area, growing cacao is almost impossible.

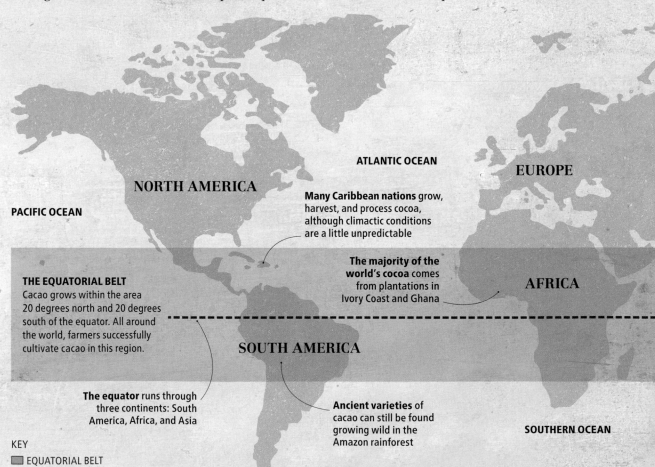

ATLANTIC OCEAN

EUROPE

NORTH AMERICA

PACIFIC OCEAN

Many Caribbean nations grow, harvest, and process cocoa, although climactic conditions are a little unpredictable

The majority of the world's cocoa comes from plantations in Ivory Coast and Ghana

AFRICA

THE EQUATORIAL BELT
Cacao grows within the area 20 degrees north and 20 degrees south of the equator. All around the world, farmers successfully cultivate cacao in this region.

SOUTH AMERICA

The equator runs through three continents: South America, Africa, and Asia

Ancient varieties of cacao can still be found growing wild in the Amazon rainforest

SOUTHERN OCEAN

KEY
■ EQUATORIAL BELT

FLOWERING TREES

One of the most distinctive features of *Theobroma cacao* is that the flowers and fruit grow directly from the trunk and larger branches. In botanical terms, this is known as "cauliflory" – papaya, jackfruit, and some varieties of fig are also cauliflory crops.

Cacao can flower and fruit all year round, usually with two distinct crops per year: a main crop and a smaller, mid crop. The timings of these harvests are determined by the local climate conditions – in some parts of the world, trees produce ripe fruit all year round.

CACAO PODS
The pods or fruit of the cacao tree grow directly from the trunk. These pods grow from a tree in Baracoa in eastern Cuba.

FLOWERING CACAO
This cacao tree in Hawaii is just beginning to flower, the tiny blossoms are no bigger than the tip of a finger.

ASIA

PACIFIC OCEAN

Cacao grows in diverse regions across Indonesia and the Philippines, and cocoa exports are rising

OCEANIA

CACAO TREES CAN BE FOUND GROWING ACROSS THE WORLD

CLOSE RELATIVE
One of cacao's closest relatives is *Theobroma grandiflorum*, known as *cupaçu*. Like cacao, cupaçu can be found throughout the Amazon basin. The fruit's pulp tastes like pear and can be juiced or used in desserts. Cupaçu seeds are ground into a paste and used to make *cupulate*, a chocolate-like confection.

CACAO VARIETIES

Cacao is genetically both diverse and difficult to classify. Traditionally, trees have been grouped into Criollo, Forastero, or Trinitario classifications. Cacao all over the world has been crossbred or cultivated to create thousands of hybrid strains. Here is an introduction to some of the best-known varieties.

DIVERSE BREEDS

Theobroma cacao is genetically diverse and readily crossbreeds to create new strains. You can find numerous different varieties even within a single plantation. Each variety may respond differently to disease, have higher or lower yields, and produce beans with differing flavour profiles. Over the years, cacao has been crossbred to bring together desirable qualities from different varieties.

Due to the sheer diversity of cacao and the oversimplified ways it has been categorized, farmers may not know precisely which varieties they have growing on their plantations. Particular varieties are associated with high-quality chocolate, although the variety of cacao is often less important than local soil and climate conditions, and the skill of the farmer and the chocolate maker. Great cacao varieties can make poor chocolate, and – in the right hands – less well-regarded varieties can produce delicious chocolate.

CHUAO
This is not technically a genetic sub-variety, but the name given to the well-known, fine-flavour beans from Chuao village in Venezuela. Strong fruity notes typify Chuao beans.

PORCELANA
Perhaps the most sought-after Criollo sub-variety, Porcelana is known for its delicate fruit flavours and distinctive appearance. Pale-coloured pods with off-white, porcelain-like beans give the variety its name.

Porcelana has pale, smooth, and rounded pods

Criollo pods are small and thin with a "warty" texture

Criollo

CRIOLLO
Often considered to produce beans of the finest flavour with rounded fruit and floral notes, the Criollo variety is named after the Spanish word for "local" or "indigenous".

DIFFERENT CACAO VARIETIES CAN BE FOUND ON THE SAME PLANTATION

ARRIBA NACIONAL
Native to Ecuador, Arriba Nacional is a prized indigenous Forestero variety. Beans from Arriba Nacional trees are renowned for their subtle floral flavours.

Trinitario pods look halfway between Criollo and Forastero in appearance

Arriba Nacional has green pods with deep furrows

TRINITARIO
Originating on the island of Trinidad in the Caribbean, Trinitario is a hybrid sub-variety. Crossbred from Criollo and Forestero, Trinitario cacao has finer flavours than Forestero and a higher yield than most Criollo.

CCN-51
A man-made hybrid created for maximum yield and disease-resistance, CCN-51 is the subject of much controversy in Ecuador and elsewhere in South America, where it is replacing native cacao varieties.

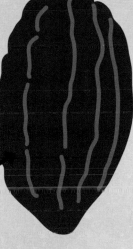

Forestero has large, rounded pods with shallow ridges

FORESTERO
Most of the world's mass-produced chocolate is made with beans from Forestero trees. This variety is high-yielding, but often lacks the finer flavours of Criollo.

GROWING CACAO

Cacao trees thrive in fertile soil and tropical climates. Growing, harvesting, and processing the beans are labour-intensive tasks that cannot easily be automated. The trees are cultivated with care, and grow for 3–5 years before they begin to flower and produce fruit.

THEOBROMA CACAO

The genus of the cacao tree is called *Theobroma*. *Theobroma cacao* is a discerning species, requiring the right conditions to grow and flower. Trees thrive in hot, humid, and relatively stable year-round conditions, requiring high humidity, slightly acidic soil, and regular rainfall to produce the best pods, and therefore the best-quality cocoa.

Cacao is sensitive to light and prefers shade. For this reason, it is usually grown under the dappled shade of taller trees – these may be other forest trees, or, most frequently, fruit trees such as banana trees. Cacao can be found growing on the edge of the rainforest, often on uneven or mountainous land.

It is labour-intensive to manage the cultivation and harvesting of cacao trees, and these tasks are difficult to automate. As a result, the crop is best suited to family-run smallholdings.

Bud

Flower

Cacao pod

PERFECT CONDITIONS

Growing environs affect the quality of the cacao, as flowers and pods are sensitive to strong winds, sunlight, and frost. Specific conditions vary around the world, but there are general conditions for cacao.

- Annual average temperature should be between 21°C (70°F) and 30°C (86°F).
- Requires dappled shade; cacao trees are often grown under taller fruit trees.
- Annual rainfall should be 1,500–2,000mm (60–80in).
- Needs slightly acidic soil (pH 5.5–7) with high nutrient levels.
- Likes high humidity levels – up to 100 per cent humidity during the day and 80 per cent humidity at night.

FROM SEED TO POD

Farmers may grow cacao from seed (the cacao bean) as shown below. Some farmers may graft seedlings onto healthy rootstock instead, to propagate a healthy and consistent crop.

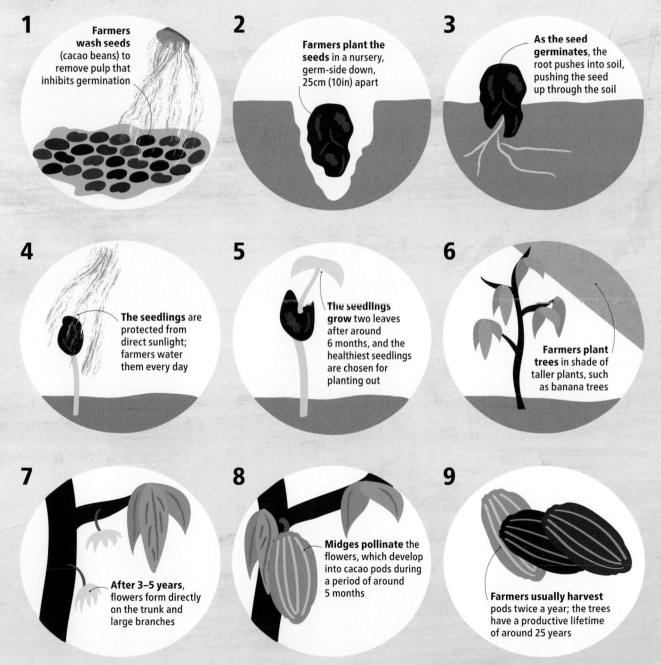

1 **Farmers wash seeds** (cacao beans) to remove pulp that inhibits germination

2 **Farmers plant the seeds** in a nursery, germ-side down, 25cm (10in) apart

3 **As the seed germinates**, the root pushes into soil, pushing the seed up through the soil

4 **The seedlings** are protected from direct sunlight; farmers water them every day

5 **The seedlings grow** two leaves after around 6 months, and the healthiest seedlings are chosen for planting out

6 **Farmers plant trees** in shade of taller plants, such as banana trees

7 **After 3–5 years**, flowers form directly on the trunk and large branches

8 **Midges pollinate** the flowers, which develop into cacao pods during a period of around 5 months

9 **Farmers usually harvest** pods twice a year; the trees have a productive lifetime of around 25 years

HARVESTING

The harvesting process involves difficult manual labour. Some cacao pods are hard to reach and farmers must take care not to damage fragile trees. It takes skill and experience to know when the pods are ripe, and how to harvest them and open them with care – all the time working as quickly as possible.

THE SEASONS

Farmers usually harvest cacao trees twice a year, in harvesting seasons that correspond to the local rainy seasons. In some parts of the world without distinct wet and dry seasons, harvesting is a perpetual year-round task.

Year-round harvesting makes the farmer's responsibilities more complex, as specific time cannot be set aside for harvesting. Fermenting small batches of beans throughout the year is more difficult than processing a few, large harvests; this presents additional problems for the farmer and chocolate maker.

FARMERS NEED TO WORK QUICKLY AND CAREFULLY TO ENJOY THE BENEFITS OF A GOOD HARVEST

THE PROCESS

Once the cacao pod is ripe, the beans inside will begin to germinate after a few weeks, so it is important to harvest quickly. Not all pods ripen at the same time, so testing and harvesting is a continuous process in peak season.

1 Testing pods for ripeness

Some skilled farmers know their trees so well that they can distinguish ripe pods by changes in colour. Others will make a small cut in the skin to look at the colour of the flesh underneath. However, the simplest way to test for ripeness is to tap the pod (see below).

TAPPING FOR RIPENESS
As the pod ripens, the beans inside become loose, giving a hollow sound when tapped or very lightly shaken.

2 Cutting the pods

When the pods are ripe, they are ready for the harvest. Farmers must take care not to damage the trees during harvesting. Future flowers, and eventually pods, will grow from the same point on the tree, so farmers must be careful not to cut the pod too close to the branch or trunk.

USING A BLADE TO HARVEST
Farmers cut hard-to-reach pods with a double-sided blade on a long pole, removing lower-hanging pods with a machete or pruning shears.

3 Opening the pods

In some parts of the world, farmers open pods with the machetes that they use for harvesting, administering a swift cut while holding the pod in the other hand. This method is dangerous and risks damaging the precious beans inside. Many farmers employ the safer method of placing the pod on a hard surface and hitting it with a blunt instrument (see left). Occasionally, farms have specialized mechanical pod-opening machines. These are rare because they are expensive and don't offer a significant increase in efficiency.

OPENING PODS WITH A BANG
Some farmers use a blunt wooden tool to open ripe cacao pods. The tools look a little like cricket bats with one angular edge.

INSIDE THE CACAO POD

Colourful and diverse in appearance, cacao pods are the fruit of the cacao tree. Each pod contains around 25–50 cacao beans, surrounded by a thick white pulp. During processing, farmers must carefully remove the soft interior from the brightly coloured outer shells, which darken to a deep brown as they age.

POD DIVERSITY

Cacao pods come in a variety of shapes, sizes, and colours. They usually range from 20–30cm (8–12in) in length and 10–15cm (4–6in) in diameter. Inside the hard outer shell of the pod, beans are arranged in rows around a central placenta, which runs along the entire length of the pod.

Different varieties and sub-varieties of cacao produce pods with contrasting appearances. From small and round to elongated and bumpy, the array of different pod styles is a reflection of the genetic diversity of cacao itself.

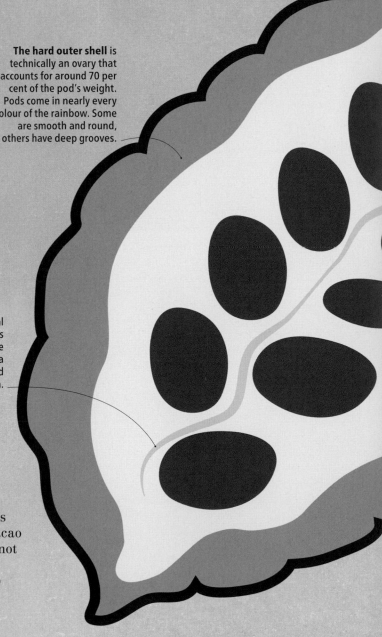

The hard outer shell is technically an ovary that accounts for around 70 per cent of the pod's weight. Pods come in nearly every colour of the rainbow. Some are smooth and round, others have deep grooves.

The placenta is the central string-like core that holds the beans together inside the pod. The placenta and pulp are liquified during fermentation.

THE CACAO POD

In botanical terms, the fruit of the cacao tree is a cherry, not a pod, although the term pod is universally accepted in the cocoa industry. Cacao pods are "indehiscent", which means they do not spontaneously burst open to release seeds. As such, farmers must open the shells by hand to process the beans inside.

THE CACAO BEAN

The seeds of the cacao pod are usually known as "beans". Once the pods are ripe, farmers must move quickly to remove the beans and pulp from the outer shell and begin fermentation, otherwise beans will begin to rot. Good-quality fresh beans are firm and surrounded by a fresh light-coloured pulp when removed from the pod.

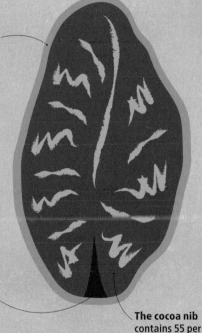

The shell (or husk) is hard, papery, and may contain traces of heavy metals, dirt, and microbes. Once the beans are processed and roasted, the shell is removed by a process called winnowing.

The germ is the central bud in the seed. It dies during the fermentation stage and this releases enzymes that enhance flavour in the cocoa.

The cocoa nib contains 55 per cent of the cocoa butter in the bean, and all of the nutritious qualities.

Cacao beans (also known as seeds) are the ovules inside the pod's ovary, and are surrounded in a sugary pulp. In the cocoa industry, they become known as cocoa beans after fermentation.

Pulp (also known as mucilage) surrounds the beans. During fermentation, yeasts grow on this sweet and tangy-tasting pulp and convert sugars to alcohol.

Roasted and winnowed nibs remain after the shell has been removed. These are the key ingredients in chocolate and cocoa-butter production.

FERMENTING AND DRYING

The first steps in developing flavour, fermenting and drying are essential aspects of the chocolate-making process. From heaps on the ground to tiered fermentation boxes, farmers use differing methods to process the wet beans into cocoa.

THE PROCESS

Once harvested, cacao must be fermented quickly. Some producers ferment the beans on the farm, but it is more common for the beans to be sent on to a local fermentation area run by a co-operative.

Traditionally, beans were simply fermented in piles on the ground, covered with banana leaves to keep the heat in. Today, most producers use slatted wooden boxes known as "sweatboxes".

The science bit

There are sugars in the pulp surrounding the beans. These sugars – glucose, fructose, and sucrose – are transformed into alcohol during fermentation. The alcohol turns into acetic acid that diffuses into the beans themselves.

The chemical reactions involved in fermentation are exothermic, meaning they produce a significant amount of heat. Temperatures inside the pile can reach 50°C (122°F) after a few days. The germ (see p35) within the bean dies from the heat, alcohol, and acetic acid produced by the pulp during fermentation. This triggers the release of enzymes within the bean. Enzymes are important for the development of chocolate flavours – these naturally occurring microorganisms kick-start the fermentation process, changing the sugars in the pulp to organic acids, and giving the beans their flavour.

1

TRANSPORTING THE BEANS
Harvested beans, still covered in pulp, are loaded into buckets and transported to a central fermentation area for processing, often mixed in with beans from neighbouring farms.

4

TURNING THE PILE
After 2–3 days, farmers turn the pile over by hand. This helps to ensure an even fermentation and introduces air into the fermentation process.

Farmers stir the pile to encourage aerobic fermentation, which turns the alcohol into acetic acid

Acetic acid is then absorbed by the beans

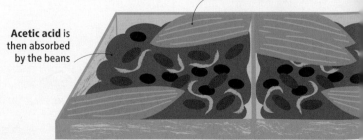

FERMENTING TECHNIQUES HAVE A REAL IMPACT ON THE FLAVOUR OF CHOCOLATE

2

TRANSFERRING TO BOXES

Farmers transfer the beans to specialized fermenting "sweatboxes", covering them with banana leaves. The boxes have gaps between the slats that are large enough for fermented pulp to drain through.

Sweatboxes are elevated off the ground so that waste pulp can run through slats in the base

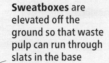

3

ANAEROBIC FERMENTATION

After the first two days of fermentation, the sugars in the pulp are converted into alcohol, producing heat and turning the pulp to liquid.

5

DRYING THE BEANS

After around 5–7 days, farmers move the beans out into the sun, often on the ground. Some farms have retractable wooden roofs that add shelter in case of rain, or greenhouse-like structures that offer protection from the elements.

6

TURNING THE BEANS

Farmers turn the beans several times a day. Many walk through the beans, furrowing them in a process known as "tramping", or use a long wooden tool called a "rabot" to turn the beans. After a week or so of drying, cocoa beans are dried and ready to be transported to makers.

SORTING THE BEANS

The chocolate maker must check cocoa beans for physical contaminants, insect damage, and signs of mould that could affect the flavour of the chocolate. They also remove any beans with holes, or any that are broken, flat, or have a significantly different colour. Depending on the size of the factory and preference, makers employ a variety of sorting methods.

SAFETY FIRST

Fermented and dried beans are usually packed into burlap sacks for transport. Cocoa beans are dried outdoors, so there is a high risk that contaminants such as twigs, stones, coffee beans, and even insects, are mixed in with the beans in the burlap sacks. Pieces of cocoa-bean germ, shell fragments, or dried pulp (see p35) may also be present. It is even possible that pieces of metal equipment or glass might make their way into the sacks.

Physically sorting the beans ensures that the chocolate is both safe to eat and tastes good. Chocolate makers employ a variety of different methods to do this.

DEFECTIVE BEANS
Craft chocolate makers remove defective-looking beans to improve the quality of chocolate. A cracked surface could be a sign that the beans have either been infested by moths, or have partially germinated.

Inspecting

Small-batch chocolate makers usually visually inspect the beans, removing unwanted objects by hand. Larger makers work with such large volumes of beans that it is impractical to solely rely on visual inspection.

Sieving

Makers use sieving to quickly remove small pieces of debris such as stones, dust, and broken pieces of bean. Beans are simply agitated over a wire mesh, allowing anything smaller than a cocoa bean to fall through.

Magnetic separation

This method is more common in larger factories. The cocoa beans are passed along a conveyor belt that takes them under strong magnets that remove any fragments of metal.

MAKERS SORT COCOA, MAKING SURE ONLY THE BEST-QUALITY BEANS REMAIN

Continuous flow

Most larger chocolate factories use automated machinery that incorporates inspecting, sieving, and magnetic separation methods into one continuous flow. Such machines often allow for grading of beans, batch by batch — the quality of a proportion of the beans is assessed to determine the final grade of each selection.

STERILIZING THE BEANS

Industrial chocolate makers will often follow the sorting process with sterilization. This usually involves briefly passing high-pressure steam over the beans. This allows enough time to kill microorganisms but not enough to cook the beans. The roasting process further sterilizes the beans, ensuring that all microorganisms are killed and the beans are safe to eat.

BURLAP SACKS
Makers usually receive cocoa beans in breathable burlap sacks, approximately 65kg (145lb) in size.

ROASTING

To get the best flavour from cocoa beans and to make sure they are safe to eat, most makers roast them in dedicated cocoa roasters, adapted commercial ovens, or coffee roasters. Makers adjust precise temperatures and timings to extract optimal flavour.

ENHANCING FLAVOUR

Roasting is a key part of the chocolate-making process, and has real impact on the flavour of cocoa. Craft makers spend a long time deciding on a roasting profile – the combination of total time and temperature – that brings out the best in the beans.

When makers receive their beans, they have been fermented and dried. The beans already look fairly dark in colour, as they will have turned a deep brown during the fermenting process, but roasting gives them evenness and texture.

There are very few machines that have been specifically designed for roasting cocoa, so small makers often have to improvise with their existing equipment.

ROASTED BEANS
In addition to boosting flavour and killing bacteria, roasting cocoa beans helps to separate the outer shell from the inner nib.

COCOA BEANS ARE SENSITIVE TO CHANGES IN TEMPERATURE, SO MAKERS MUST MONITOR THEM CAREFULLY

The science bit

Named after the French physician and chemist Louis Camille Maillard, the Maillard Reaction gives roasted cocoa beans their distinctive flavour and aroma. The chemical process happens when the beans reach approximately 140ºC (275ºF) under dry heat, at which point sugars and amino acids reducing in the beans react. Other examples of the Maillard Reaction include the flavour development of roasted meat and the crust on baked bread.

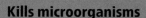

Why roast?

Kills microorganisms
Makers usually roast cocoa beans in temperatures of between 120°C (225°F)–140°C (275°F) for 15–30 minutes. This kills microorganisms such as bacteria on the outer shell, effectively sterilizing the beans.

Loosens the outer shell
Cocoa beans have a papery outer shell that must be removed before they can be made into chocolate (see pp42–43). Roasting helps to dry and loosen this shell so that it is easier to remove.

Develops flavour
Roasting cocoa beans helps to develop their natural flavour. Chocolate makers may conduct tests at different temperatures until the beans have reached a consistent flavour profile.

How do makers roast?

Coffee roaster
Cocoa beans are roasted at lower temperatures to coffee beans, but modified coffee roasters are often used by medium–large chocolate makers. Once roasted, beans are placed on a cooling tray to halt the process.

Conventional commercial oven
Many makers use commercial ovens or even bread ovens to roast the beans. Sometimes ovens are modified with internal rotating drums to ensure an even roast of every bean.

BREAKING AND WINNOWING

Before roasted beans can be ground into chocolate, makers crush the beans and then separate the nibs from their papery, inedible shells in a process known as breaking and winnowing. Methods vary, but most makers use machines that undertake both tasks, as simplified below.

BREAKING

The roasting process dries cocoa beans and loosens their shells – this means that very little needs to be done to separate the two. Most makers separate nibs from shells by breaking the beans. Roasted beans are fed through metal rollers. Gravity forces the beans through the narrow gap between the rollers, breaking the beans into pieces of nib and shell.

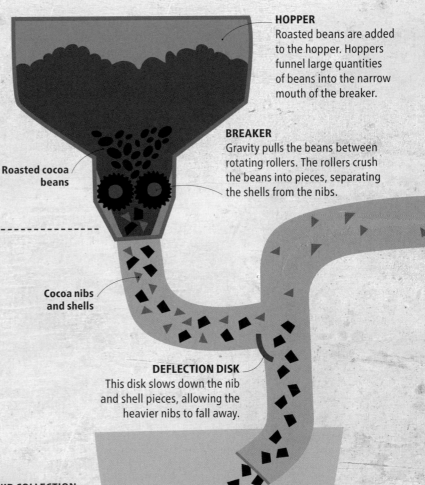

HOPPER
Roasted beans are added to the hopper. Hoppers funnel large quantities of beans into the narrow mouth of the breaker.

Roasted cocoa beans

BREAKER
Gravity pulls the beans between rotating rollers. The rollers crush the beans into pieces, separating the shells from the nibs.

WINNOWING

The broken, intermingled pieces of nib and shell are separated out by winnowing. Winnowing machines use airflow – usually a vacuum – to suck or blow away the waste pieces of shell. The broken beans are dropped into the machine. The lighter shells are sucked through the machine by a vacuum pump, while the heavier nibs fall away into a separate container or compartments. The waste shells can be composted or used as mulch, while the nibs go on to become chocolate.

Cocoa nibs and shells

DEFLECTION DISK
This disk slows down the nib and shell pieces, allowing the heavier nibs to fall away.

NIB COLLECTION
The winnowed nibs are collected, ready to be ground into chocolate.

Clean cocoa nibs

CLEAN COCOA NIBS CONTAIN ALL THE FLAVOUR OF FERMENTED AND ROASTED COCOA

CLEAN COCOA NIBS
Once cocoa beans have been broken and winnowed, only the cocoa nibs remain.

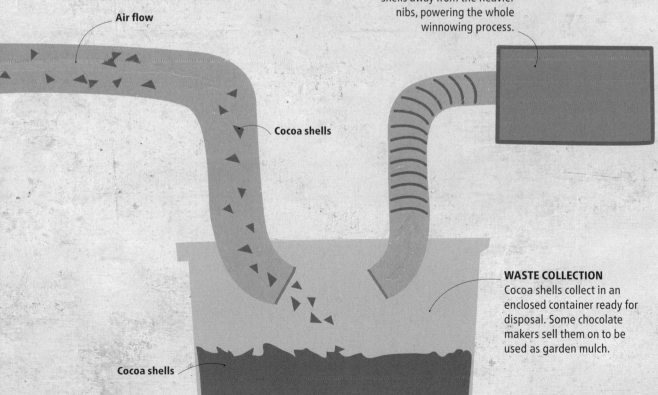

VACUUM PUMP
Suction from the vacuum pump pulls the lighter cocoa shells away from the heavier nibs, powering the whole winnowing process.

Air flow

Cocoa shells

WASTE COLLECTION
Cocoa shells collect in an enclosed container ready for disposal. Some chocolate makers sell them on to be used as garden mulch.

Cocoa shells

GRINDING AND REFINING

To transform roasted cocoa nibs into chocolate, nibs are ground down into a liquid cocoa mass known as "cocoa liquor". Makers add sugar and cocoa butter, milk powder (if making milk chocolate), and any powdered flavourings or "inclusions". The mixture is then refined to create the smooth mouthfeel we expect from chocolate.

CREATING THE RIGHT TEXTURE

To transform cocoa nibs into liquid cocoa mass, nibs must be finely ground until the particles have a diameter of less than 30 microns, or 0.03mm ($\frac{1}{800}$ in). At this size, individual cocoa particles are almost imperceptible to the tongue, so we perceive the chocolate to have a silky, smooth texture. Chocolate makers use a variety of machines to accomplish the grinding and refining process (see opposite).

ADDING INGREDIENTS
Small-scale chocolate makers often add sugar at the refining stage, along with milk powder if they are making milk chocolate. Larger manufacturers will often produce what is known as a "milk crumb" first, by combining condensed milk with cocoa mass and sugar, before milling the mixture to a fine powder. This powder can then be heated and combined with additional cocoa butter to produce a liquid chocolate.

COCOA NIBS
Nibs are naturally bitter and acidic-tasting, so makers add sugar and other ingredients to them to balance out the flavour profile.

LIQUID CHOCOLATE
After several hours of grinding and refining, hard, solid cocoa nibs become smooth, liquid chocolate.

PRE-GRINDING
Some small grinding machines have difficulty processing large pieces of cocoa nib, so makers can pre-grind the nibs to make them easier to work with. Nut grinders, such as those used to make peanut butter, are often used to coarsely grind the nibs to a thick paste.

COCOA NIBS ARE GROUND AND REFINED TO FORM SMOOTH, LIQUID CHOCOLATE

MELANGER

Favoured by chocolate makers for more than a hundred years, melangers are one of the simplest machines for grinding and refining chocolate. Smaller makers also use them for conching (see pp46–47). Two granite wheels rotate over a granite base, repeatedly forcing the cocoa mass between the granite stones to smooth the texture.

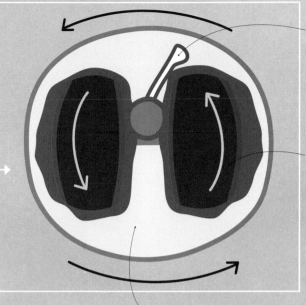

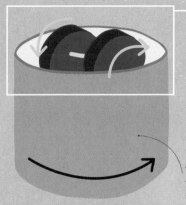

The scraper keeps the cocoa mass moving through the system, channelling it back towards the wheels to be continually ground and refined

The granite wheels rotate in opposite directions, moving with the base to reduce the particle size of the cocoa mass and improve the texture of the liquid chocolate

The outer drum rotates around the inner wheels, powering the movement of the cocoa mass

The granite base rotates with the outer drum, creating friction with the wheels; this energy helps to melt the nibs into cocoa mass

ROLL REFINER

Larger chocolate makers tend to favour roll refiners – they are more expensive, but also more efficient. Roll refiners force cocoa mass between a series of large metal rollers, gradually refining it as it passes from roller to roller.

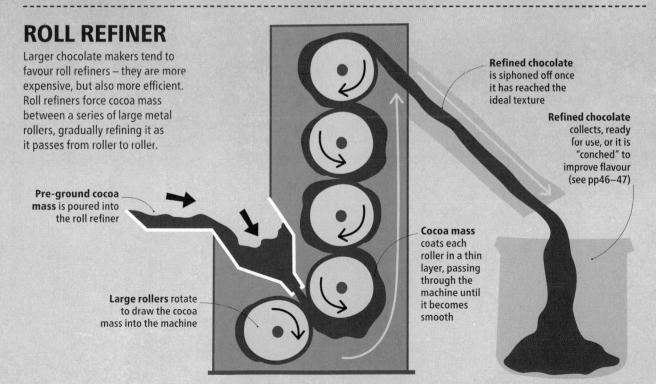

Pre-ground cocoa mass is poured into the roll refiner

Large rollers rotate to draw the cocoa mass into the machine

Cocoa mass coats each roller in a thin layer, passing through the machine until it becomes smooth

Refined chocolate is siphoned off once it has reached the ideal texture

Refined chocolate collects, ready for use, or it is "conched" to improve flavour (see pp46–47)

CONCHING

Once chocolate has been refined to the optimal texture, makers heat and stir it to further develop flavour. This process is called "conching", and takes a few hours to several days, depending on the cocoa beans and the preferences of the maker. The chocolate mixture can conche in melangers, but large makers use specialized conching machines.

ORIGINS OF THE CONCHE

The chocolate conching machine was invented in 1879 by Swiss chocolate maker Rodolphe Lindt. It was named a "conching machine" because the basin containing the chocolate was shaped like a conche shell. Lindt's machine used a simple roller to move the chocolate back and forth, while heating it from below. Modern conching machines work on the same principle, using wheels or paddles to agitate the liquid chocolate and develop the flavour of the finished product.

Today, many smaller chocolate makers forgo a separate conching machine, relying purely on melangers (see pp44–45) to grind, refine, and then conche their chocolate. Some medium-sized makers build their own conching machine, as very few manufacturers produce chocolate-making equipment of the right scale. Larger chocolate manufacturers use industrial-scale conching machines (see below) that are able to heat, mix, and monitor several tonnes of chocolate at once.

CONCHED CHOCOLATE
Once chocolate has been conched, it should have a rounded, developed flavour with little acidity or astringency. It can be left to age, or tempered and used immediately.

SWISS INVENTION

Rodolphe Lindt's conching machine was similar to the equipment that large-scale chocolate makers use today: Liquid chocolate is poured into a large, curved basin, and a metal roller agitates the chocolate by moving backwards and forwards in a rolling pin-like motion. A heated granite slab warms the liquid chocolate from below, ensuring an even conching process.

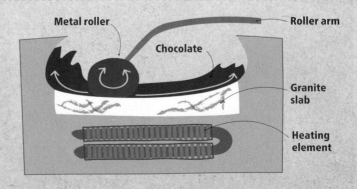

Metal roller

Roller arm

Chocolate

Granite slab

Heating element

The science bit

Chocolate makers know that conching has a beneficial impact on chocolate, but the chemistry of the process is still not fully understood. Friction and heat create changes in the cocoa particles that improve the flavour of the chocolate.

Heat and movement help reduce levels of astringent- and bitter-tasting elements in the chocolate.

Residual moisture – a natural enemy of chocolate – evaporates away during conching.

Cocoa particles become evenly coated with cocoa butter, improving the texture of the chocolate.

Some conching machines continue to refine chocolate, further reducing particle size.

THE CONCHING PROCESS
The friction of the granite wheels in this melanger creates heat to conche chocolate – this action is very similar to the movement of metal rollers in traditional conching machines.

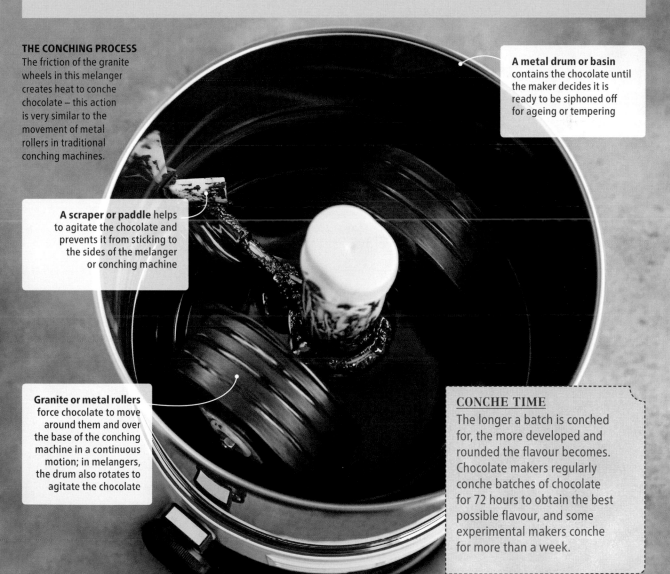

A metal drum or basin contains the chocolate until the maker decides it is ready to be siphoned off for ageing or tempering

A scraper or paddle helps to agitate the chocolate and prevents it from sticking to the sides of the melanger or conching machine

Granite or metal rollers force chocolate to move around them and over the base of the conching machine in a continuous motion; in melangers, the drum also rotates to agitate the chocolate

CONCHE TIME
The longer a batch is conched for, the more developed and rounded the flavour becomes. Chocolate makers regularly conche batches of chocolate for 72 hours to obtain the best possible flavour, and some experimental makers conche for more than a week.

TEMPERING

Chocolate makers temper chocolate to give it a glossy finish and distinctive "snap" sound when it is broken. Tempering is an important process that improves the appearance and texture of chocolate. It is a slow process by hand, so makers use machines that accurately heat and cool chocolate.

THE THREE STAGES

Tempering is a physical process that alters the crystal structure in chocolate so that it hardens to the perfect texture. The technique involves heating and cooling chocolate to three precise temperatures – these temperatures vary according to whether it is dark, milk, or white chocolate (see p151).

Tempering involves three stages – the first stage is to destroy the existing crystal structure in the chocolate, the second is to allow the structure to reform, and the third is to destroy all crystal types except for one, type V, which has the perfect properties (see right).

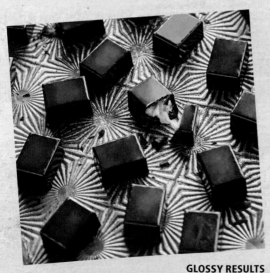

GLOSSY RESULTS
Chocolate makers temper chocolate to give chocolates and bars a shiny finish and the correct melting temperature.

The science bit

Cocoa butter is polymorphic, which means it can exist in several different crystal formations. There are six crystal types in cocoa butter, and tempering destroys types I–IV, leaving type V behind. Type VI crystals are not formed during the tempering process – these crystals only develop from Type V after very long periods of storage.

TYPE OF CRYSTAL	MELTING POINT	CHOCOLATE PROPERTIES
VI	36°C (97°F)	Hard, melts too slowly
V	34°C (93°F)	Glossy with good snap; melts just below body temperature
IV	27°C (81°F)	Firm, good snap, but melts too readily
III	25°C (77°F)	Firm, but poor snap and melts too readily
II	23°C (73°F)	Soft and crumbly
I	17°C (63°F)	Soft and crumbly

THE EQUIPMENT

Chocolatiers temper chocolate by hand using a marble slab, but that method is not suitable for large batches of chocolate, so chocolate makers frequently use tempering machines. There are many varieties of machine – some medium-scale chocolate makers temper chocolate in rotating bowl machines (see right). Larger-scale chocolate makers may use the more advanced continuous tempering machines (see below).

THE ROTATING BOWL TEMPERING MACHINE
Chocolate melts in a gently rotating bowl in this machine, and is then either heated by an element or cooled by a fan to reach precise temperatures.

THE CONTINUOUS TEMPERING MACHINE

Easily programmed to specific temperatures, continuous tempering machines circulate chocolate around a system using a screw-pump. Tempered chocolate is released through a dosing head that can be set to deliver precisely the right quantity.

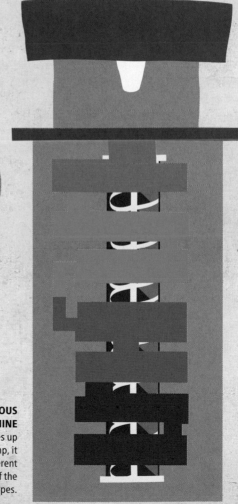

1

The basin is the entry point for melted chocolate, which travels to the bottom of the machine to the screw-pump

2

The heating element heats chocolate in the screw-pump to a precise temperature

3
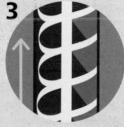
The screw-pump moves chocolate continuously upwards through temperature zones

4
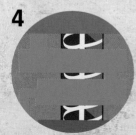
Cooling pipes, filled with refrigerated liquid, cool chocolate to the exact temperature required

5

The dosing head releases tempered chocolate; unused chocolate falls into the basin and flows back into the system

THE CONTINUOUS TEMPERING MACHINE
As the chocolate moves up through the screw-pump, it moves through the different temperature zones of the surrounding pipes.

MOULDING AND WRAPPING

Once it is tempered, chocolate must be transferred into moulds immediately before it starts to cool and set. Presentation is key: from the size and shape of the moulds to the style of the packaging, every aspect of the design should increase the consumer's anticipation for the chocolate inside.

DESIGN MATTERS

A chocolate maker or chocolatier will often have their own signature mould for their truffles, filled chocolates, and bars. Once the chocolate is set and cooled, it is ready for wrapping. Packaging designers play a key role in how chocolate products are presented and marketed. Craft chocolate bars, in particular, have gained a reputation for having attractive, contemporary wrapping, as makers seek to display their artisan, small-scale credentials. However, small makers often find that packaging is a time-consuming process, because they need to wrap by hand.

KEEPING IT FRESH

Many makers choose to wrap chocolate bars in foil, as it is a protective wrapper for bars and filled chocolates. Foil is usually encased in a paper or card outer wrapping. Resealable boxes or pouches are also popular, as they are equally protective and keep chocolate fresh for longer.

Foil gives chocolate bars an attractive finish, but it takes skill and practice to wrap neatly by hand

Good-quality card, featuring modern designs, is often used to package craft bars

WRAPPED CHOCOLATE BARS
Design plays a key role in how we perceive chocolate products, so makers and chocolatiers invest money in beautiful, distinctive packaging.

AIR BUBBLES

Trapped inside moulds during the making process, air bubbles mar the appearance of bars and filled chocolates. To dislodge bubbles before chocolate sets, makers place filled moulds on mechanized vibrating plates or conveyor belts. Smaller makers simply tap each mould by hand until the bubbles disperse.

LARGE SCALE

Large chocolate makers may use wrapping machines, which can significantly increase the speed of wrapping. The most common machines are called flow-wrapping machines – these use a continuous sheet of plastic to seal individual bars. Chocolate makers might also use computer-controlled dosing machines that fill moulds precisely with tempered chocolate.

PACKAGING DESIGN PLAYS A KEY ROLE IN OUR BUYING DECISIONS

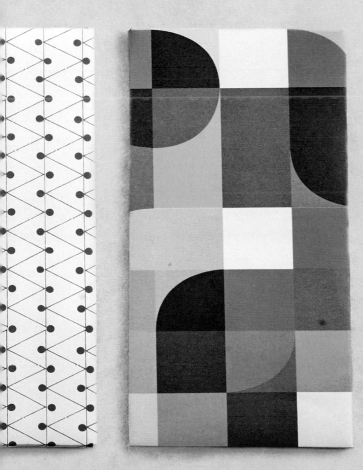

PRODUCTION LINE
Continuous computer-controlled dosing machines precisely fill moulds, and then lightly vibrate them on mechanized conveyor belts to dislodge air bubbles.

TEMPERING MACHINE
Large tempering machines (see p49) can temper batches of 550kg (1200lb) chocolate per hour. Makers manage the flow of chocolate with a foot pedal.

COMMODITY TRADE

Cocoa has been traded as an international commodity for hundreds of years – bought and sold at a fixed price regardless of origin or quality. There is a long chain of people involved in commodity trading, meaning that much of the price of cocoa beans has been absorbed by traders, processors, and government taxes before farmers receive their cut.

THE INDUSTRIAL SCALE

Around 95 per cent of chocolate produced around the world is made on an industrial scale in very large factories. These few large manufacturers dominate the commodity trade, and prepare chocolate and couverture before selling it to makers (confectionery companies, chocolatiers, and pastry chefs), rather than selling it directly to the public. As a result, you may never have heard of some of the biggest manufacturers in the chocolate industry.

Chocolate manufacturers such as Barry Callebaut, Cargill, ADM, and Belcolade and the more well-known brands Nestlé, Mondelez (formerly Kraft), and Mars produce chocolate on an industrial scale. They rely on being able to obtain cocoa in large quantities, so most of the cocoa used in industrial manufacture comes from Ivory Coast and Ghana, where beans are largely grown for maximum yield rather than flavour.

GIANTS OF CHOCOLATE

Many large-scale chocolate manufacturers started as small family businesses in the 19th century. Through a combination of growth and acquisitions, they have become giants. This is particularly evident in European countries such as Belgium – a country synonymous with chocolate. Once home to many independent chocolate makers, the country's industry is now dominated by industrial chocolate manufacturers, producing Belgian chocolate for confectionery companies around the world.

MOST CHOCOLATE IS CREATED BY A SMALL NUMBER OF BIG BRANDS

The process of making chocolate on an industrial scale is largely the same as smaller-scale production, with every stage optimized for efficiency. Factories reduce costs and the need for human intervention with giant roasters, conching machines with the capacity of several tonnes, and wrapping machines that can wrap hundreds of bars per minute.

SOURCING COUVERTURE
Many chocolatiers create truffles and filled chocolates using couverture made by large-scale chocolate manufacturers.

THE COMMODITY TRADE CHAIN

Most of the world's cocoa goes through many trade channels between the farmer and the finished chocolate bar. Here is a typical journey of cocoa beans from a farm in West Africa to a large confectionery chocolate maker.

Cocoa farmers
1 grow, harvest, ferment, and dry cocoa beans

Exporters buy
beans in bulk,
4 grading them
and packing
them for export

Regional
wholesalers buy
3 beans from the
small traders

Small traders
2 visit many
farms, buying
cocoa beans

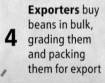

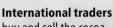

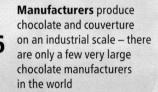

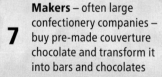

International traders
buy and sell the cocoa
as a commodity; cocoa
5 is shipped in bulk to
manufacturer factories,
and stored ready to be
made into chocolate

Manufacturers produce
chocolate and couverture
on an industrial scale – there
6 are only a few very large
chocolate manufacturers
in the world

Makers – often large
confectionery companies –
buy pre-made couverture
7 chocolate and transform it
into bars and chocolates

DIRECT TRADE

The system of direct trade has become more common in recent years, particularly with craft makers. In most direct-trade transactions, makers buy cocoa directly from farmers or co-operatives. This relationship ensures that farmers receive a fair price for their product, and that makers can work closely with farmers to optimize quality and flavour.

THE DIRECT TRADE CHAIN

The journey of directly traded cocoa varies considerably according to the origins of the beans and the preference of farmers. Some cocoa farmers communicate directly with makers and use export brokers to handle distribution.

The supply chain is much shorter than the commodity trade chain (see p53) and this means that cacao farmers receive a larger cut for their crop, and can afford to improve working conditions and processing techniques.

The below chain is a generalized version of the direct-trade journey from a cacao-growing country to the craft chocolate maker.

1 **Cocoa farmers** grow, harvest, ferment, and dry cocoa beans, and join forces with a co-operative

2 **Co-operatives or small traders** work with exporters or export cocoa beans directly to makers

3 **Makers** buy processed cocoa beans and transform them into bars, giving feedback on the quality where appropriate

DIRECT RELATIONSHIP

Direct trade cuts out the middlemen, so chocolate makers are able to pay significantly more for cocoa. In some cases, makers pay five times more than the Fairtrade price for fine-flavoured cocoa beans (see opposite).

The direct relationship means the maker can give feedback on the quality of the beans and perhaps give advice on how fermentation or drying processes could be improved. Farmers

also have a vested interest in making sure their beans get the best possible treatment from the moment they're harvested.

TRACEABILITY

Perhaps the biggest advantage of direct trade is that of traceability. Chocolate made with directly traded beans can be easily traced back to the original farm – a detail that is usually impossible in the commodity trade.

WHAT IS FAIRTRADE?

Around 0.5 per cent of cocoa on the market today is certified as Fairtrade. The Fairtrade Foundation is a leading fair-trading partnership that offers farmers a premium for their product with the aim of providing better conditions and pay for farmers.

What does the Fairtrade logo mean?

When you see the Fairtrade logo, it signifies that producers have met social, economic, and environmental standards, that labour conditions are fair, and that a minimum price and premium have been paid for the ingredients.

Why is it important?

In some countries, the average age of a cocoa farmer is greater than the average life expectancy. It's vital that the industry invests in the future and that money gets back to people who need it the most – the farmers in some of the poorest parts of the world.

What do cocoa farmers receive?

Traders pay 10 per cent over the market rate for Fairtrade cocoa, and producers are also entitled to a Fairtrade Premium, which currently works out as £100 (US$150) per tonne of cocoa. However, farmers must also pay a fee to become Fairtrade-certified.

What's not to like?

The Fairtrade Foundation system means that companies can use non-certified cocoa in Fairtrade-labelled products if they have purchased an equivalent quantity of certified beans for other products. As a result, it is possible that a bar marked as Fairtrade may contain no Fairtrade beans at all.

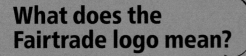

EXPLORE

Cacao trees thrive in the nutrient-rich soil and tropical climate of the equatorial belt. Take a tour of each growing region, discovering the stories, traditions, and challenges behind the beans.

IVORY COAST

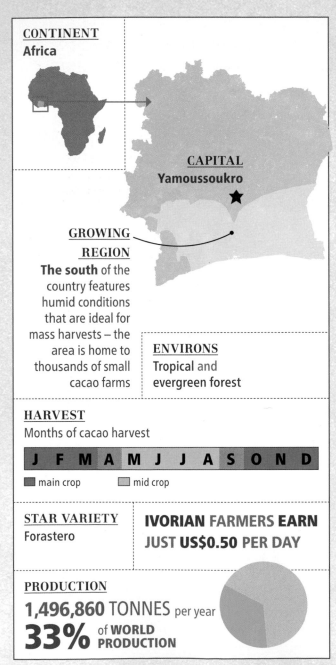

CONTINENT
Africa

CAPITAL
Yamoussoukro

GROWING REGION
The south of the country features humid conditions that are ideal for mass harvests – the area is home to thousands of small cacao farms

ENVIRONS
Tropical and evergreen forest

HARVEST
Months of cacao harvest

| J | F | M | A | M | J | J | A | S | O | N | D |

■ main crop   ■ mid crop

STAR VARIETY
Forastero

IVORIAN FARMERS **EARN** JUST **US$0.50** PER DAY

PRODUCTION
1,496,860 TONNES per year
33% of **WORLD PRODUCTION**

Since gaining independence from France in 1960, cocoa production in Ivory Coast has boomed – the country now exports more cocoa beans than any other nation.

Cacao first became a major crop in Ivory Coast during the late 1800s, when French colonizers sought to maximize their profits in the region. This trend towards high-yield, lower-quality beans continues today – cacao is grown for maximum production at minimum cost.

GROWING IN BULK

Nearly all the cocoa produced here is used to make mass-produced confectionery chocolate. Recent dry conditions brought about by climate change have created a real challenge for farmers, as they mean higher production costs and lower yields from cacao trees. As farmers struggle to make a living from cacao, confectionery companies face a shortage of the bulk-grown cocoa beans required to mass-produce chocolate.

CHALLENGES FOR FARMERS

Growing takes place mainly on small family farms. Farmers grow and often ferment their own beans before drying them in central drying areas. From there, buyers purchase the dried beans and transport them to warehouses in large towns and cities. This long chain of production results in very little money filtering down to the growers, so making a living can be challenging.

Growers' co-operatives, such as the Entreprise Coopérative Kimbre (ECOOKIM), pool resources to market and sell their members' cocoa more efficiently. Such organizations are especially vital in a country where forced labour and child labour are still nationwide problems.

GHANA

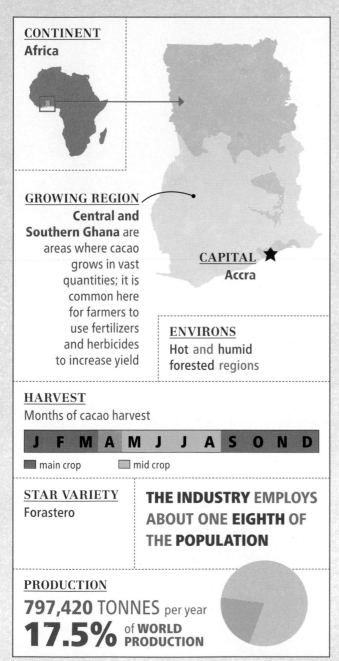

CONTINENT
Africa

GROWING REGION
Central and Southern Ghana are areas where cacao grows in vast quantities; it is common here for farmers to use fertilizers and herbicides to increase yield

CAPITAL ★
Accra

ENVIRONS
Hot and humid forested regions

HARVEST
Months of cacao harvest

J	F	M	A	M	J	J	A	S	O	N	D

■ main crop   ■ mid crop

STAR VARIETY
Forastero

THE INDUSTRY EMPLOYS ABOUT ONE **EIGHTH** OF THE **POPULATION**

PRODUCTION
797,420 TONNES per year
17.5% of **WORLD PRODUCTION**

The world's second-largest cocoa producer, after neighbouring country Ivory Coast, Ghana produces bulk-grown cocoa for use in confectionery chocolate.

There are differing explanations for the arrival of cacao in Ghana. Some believe that it was first introduced by Dutch missionaries, while others attribute the spread of the crop to Tetteh Quarshie, a Ghanaian agriculturalist who brought cacao beans back from Equatorial Guinea in the late 1800s.

THE FARMER'S LIFE
Today, large quantities of the crop grow in six of Ghana's ten regions: Western, Central, Brong Ahafo, Eastern, Ashanti, and Volta. Cocoa is now the country's main export, although production has fallen in recent years due to challenging conditions for farmers. Economic and environmental issues are taking their toll on the industry, making life tough for the average Ghanaian cocoa farmer.

ALL COCOA IS SOLD AT A FIXED PRICE

Operational costs have increased more than the price paid to growers for their beans – and as 90 per cent of Ghanaian cacao is grown by smallholders, these disparities have made it very hard for them to stay in business. However, in part due to centralized control of cocoa exports by the Ghana Cocoa Board, Ghanaian farmers make more money than their Ivorian neighbours – US$0.84 per day compared to US$0.50 per day.

MADAGASCAR

Although Madagascar harvests less than one per cent of the world's cocoa per year, the island nation is famous for producing fine-flavoured, intensely fruity chocolate – the jewel in Africa's cacao-growing crown.

Originally introduced to Madagascar in the 1800s, cacao thrived under French colonial rule in the early 19th century. The distinctively fruity, fine-flavoured cocoa beans grown on the island today are used primarily to make high-end, craft chocolate.

**CONTINENT
Africa**

CHOCOLATERIE ROBERT AND CINAGRA

Madagascar is a rare case in the cocoa industry because beans are grown, harvested, and also processed into chocolate within the country. There are two chocolate factories on the island, each producing bars and confections from cocoa beans grown in the Sambirano Valley. Chocolaterie Robert was founded in the 1940s in the capital Antananarivo, using beans from nearby farms to create chocolate primarily for the local market. Robert now produces the Chocolat Madagascar brand and sells it all over the world.

Cinagra, the second factory, produces the award-winning Menakao range of bars for the international market. Menakao chocolate is made using only Malagasy ingredients, including flavourings such as coconut and pink pepper.

DRYING THE BEANS
Farmers rotate the beans as they dry naturally in the sun at the Ambolikapiky plantation in the Sambirano Valley.

DISTINCTIVE TASTES

Madagascan chocolate's naturally sweet and uniquely fruity flavour notes make it a favourite of chocolate makers and chocolatiers around the world. It is often paired with fruit-flavoured fillings or a touch of salt to enhance the citrus and sweet flavours.

MADAG

MADA

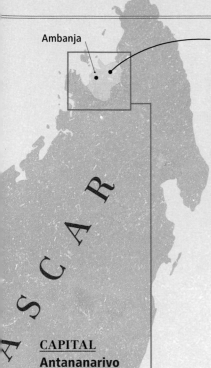

Ambanja

GROWING REGION
Sambirano Valley
is a relatively small
region in northern
Madagascar, but
almost all of the
island's cacao is grown
there, within 80km
(50 miles) of the city
of Ambanja

CAPITAL
Antananarivo
★

Ambanja

KEY PLANTATION
Ambolikapiky is a
2,000-hectare (5,000-acre)
plantation run by Bertil Åkesson;
it produces high-quality beans
for the best chocolate makers,
including Åkesson's Organic

ENVIRONS
Cacao grows in **naturally fertile river valleys**

THERE ARE 15,000 HECTARES (37,000 ACRES) OF CACAO FARMS ON THE ISLAND. THE COUNTRY ALSO HARVESTS VANILLA, COFFEE, AND SUGAR CANE

HARVEST
Months of cacao harvest

| J | F | M | A | M | J | J | A | S | O | N | D |

■ main crop ■ mid crop

CACAO IS GROWN ON SMALL FAMILY FARMS, MANY OF WHICH WERE ONCE FRUIT PLANTATIONS WHEN THE ISLAND WAS UNDER FRENCH COLONIAL RULE

STAR VARIETIES
Criollo and Trinitario

FLAVOUR NOTES
Fruity and naturally sweet,
with notes of citrus

MADAGASCAR IS FAMOUS FOR VANILLA PODS AS WELL AS CACAO – THE TWO ARE OFTEN COMBINED IN CHOCOLATE BARS

PRODUCTION
7,260 TONNES per year
0.16% of **WORLD PRODUCTION**

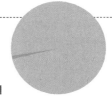

TANZANIA

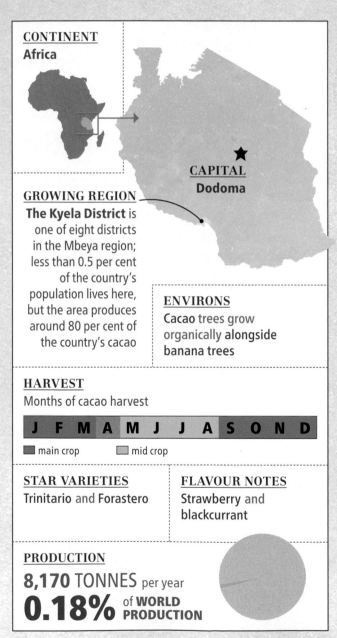

CONTINENT
Africa

CAPITAL
Dodoma

GROWING REGION
The Kyela District is one of eight districts in the Mbeya region; less than 0.5 per cent of the country's population lives here, but the area produces around 80 per cent of the country's cacao

ENVIRONS
Cacao trees grow organically **alongside** banana trees

HARVEST
Months of cacao harvest

J	F	M	A	M	J	J	A	S	O	N	D

■ main crop   ■ mid crop

STAR VARIETIES
Trinitario and Forastero

FLAVOUR NOTES
Strawberry and blackcurrant

PRODUCTION
8,170 TONNES per year
0.18% of **WORLD PRODUCTION**

Tanzania's cocoa industry is neither as established nor as organized as some of its better-known African neighbours, but in recent years the country has made a name for itself as a producer of fine cocoa.

Not widely known for cocoa production, Tanzania produces a relatively small quantity of cocoa that has become increasingly popular with the world's craft chocolate makers. The Trinitario cocoa beans from the Mbeya region feature subtle and fruity flavour notes.

INVESTING IN QUALITY

Most farmers in Tanzania still operate independently, rather than as part of a co-operative. When farmers sell their produce this puts them at a disadvantage, and it means that they cannot benefit from shared knowledge and resources. However, with backing from the Tanzanian government and the support of international craft chocolate makers, the quality and quantity of Tanzania's cocoa is improving every year.

WORKING IN PARTNERSHIP

The American chocolate maker Shawn Askinosie has been working with farmers in the Kyela District since 2010. His direct relationship with the farmers not only helps to produce better chocolate, but also forms part of a wider educational programme that gives American students the opportunity to meet and work with Tanzanian farmers and students. The chocolate they produce together accentuates the delicate berry flavours of the local cocoa.

DEMOCRATIC REPUBLIC OF CONGO (DRC)

The Democratic Republic of Congo produces cocoa that is used to make premium chocolate with a fine and fruity flavour. In one of the poorest and most politically volatile countries in Africa, cocoa production provides hope for many.

The majority of the country's cacao crop is grown in the northeastern region – an area known for rich biodiversity and violence in equal measure.

GIVING FARMS A LIFELINE

Fruit from the cacao tree is difficult to process, so it has little value to the militia in the region, who are more likely to steal other crops. With proper management, farmers are able to achieve a premium price for their crop. Most people who live in this area are subsistence farmers, so cocoa is becoming a vital product and is helping to slowly transform lives – a real step forward for a country that has one of the lowest GDP per capita rates in the world.

CACAO IS HELPING TO CHANGE LIVES

In recent years, education and reforestation initiatives involving craft chocolate companies such as Theo Chocolate and Original Beans have helped to stimulate the DRC's cocoa industry, placing Congolese produce on the map. In 2011, Original Beans won an Academy of Chocolate Award for its Cru Virunga bar, proving the potential of Congolese cocoa.

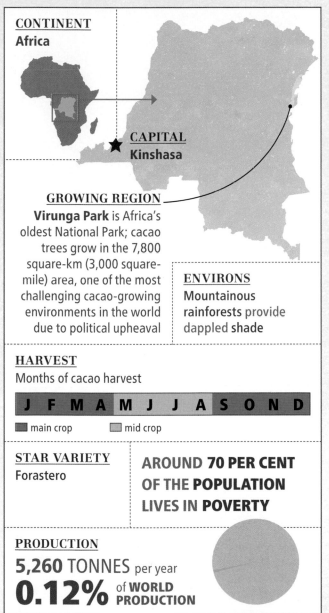

CONTINENT
Africa

CAPITAL
Kinshasa

GROWING REGION
Virunga Park is Africa's oldest National Park; cacao trees grow in the 7,800 square-km (3,000 square-mile) area, one of the most challenging cacao-growing environments in the world due to political upheaval

ENVIRONS
Mountainous rainforests provide dappled shade

HARVEST
Months of cacao harvest

| J | F | M | A | M | J | J | A | S | O | N | D |

■ main crop   ■ mid crop

STAR VARIETY
Forastero

AROUND 70 PER CENT OF THE POPULATION LIVES IN POVERTY

PRODUCTION
5,260 TONNES per year
0.12% of WORLD PRODUCTION

Behind the scenes | The Original
Hawaiian Chocolate Factory

THE TREE-TO-BAR MAKER

Based in the Kona region of Hawaii's Big Island, The Original Hawaiian Chocolate Factory produces chocolate made from 100 per cent Hawaiian cocoa beans. The small team controls every stage of the chocolate-making process, ensuring good-quality, flavour-rich results.

Employs 10 people: 3 on the farm and 7 in the factory and shop

----

Moved to Hawaii from North Carolina in 1997

Created the first batch of chocolate in 2000

The company's founders, Pam and Bob Cooper, make chocolate on their 2.5-hectare (6-acre) farm on Hawaii's Big Island. The couple moved from mainland US in 1997 and bought a farm with coffee, macadamia nut, and cacao trees. Without any agricultural experience, they started to make some uniquely Hawaiian chocolate in their own back garden. There was no access to small-batch commercial chocolate-making equipment in Hawaii then, so they sourced it from Europe and mainland US or had it custom-made.

The Coopers grow and process chocolate, keeping everything local. They have control over each step of the process, ensuring a fine-quality 100 per cent tree-to-bar product. As well as using their own cacao beans, they also source them from 10–15 local growers.

The company's vision is for Hawaii to become the "Napa Valley" of cacao-growing and chocolate-making in the US.

CHOCOLATE CHALLENGES

The biggest challenge in Hawaii is the tropical weather. If there is no rain within a 10-day period, the farmers have to irrigate the trees. Strong winds and temperatures that occasionally

drop below 10°C (50°F) have a detrimental effect on tree health. The beans need sunshine to dry, so the team must constantly monitor the weather. The chocolate is packaged and stored in a controlled environment that monitors temperature and humidity.

A DAY IN THE LIFE

Each day on the farm has a specific function. Cacao pod-harvesting happens on Mondays; bar-moulding happens on Tuesdays and Thursdays; Pam and Bob offer plantation tours on Wednesdays and Fridays; and Saturdays are for accounting duties and chocolate-making in the factory. This leaves Sunday as a rest day.

TURNING THE BEANS
Farmers turn cocoa beans two or three times a day to ensure they dry at an even rate under the heat of the sun.

DRYING BEANS
The beans are dried on small raised platforms with lids to protect them from Hawaii's frequent rain.

TEMPERING MACHINE
Chocolate is tempered in specialized equipment in the on-site factory, some of which has to be air-conditioned due to the climate.

CACAO RAINBOW
Cacao pods from the trees on the Coopers' farm ripen to every colour of the rainbow.

DOMINICAN REPUBLIC

After early experiments by Spanish _conquistadores_, cacao-growing was introduced to the Dominican Republic by the French in 1665.

Today the country is the second-poorest in the Caribbean, and cocoa is a key source of income for small-scale producers. The amount of land devoted to cacao-farming has more than doubled in the last 40 years, due to increasing demand and investment from American and European chocolate companies.

FERMENTING FOR FLAVOUR

All cocoa grown and processed in the Dominican Republic is of the Trinitario variety, but farmers produce two different grades of cocoa beans – Sanchez and Hispaniola beans.

Farmers dry Sanchez beans immediately after harvesting, making them quick and cheap to produce but meaning they lack complex flavours that develop over time. These beans are used to produce cocoa butter or confectionery chocolate.

Hispaniola beans are fermented for 5–7 days before being left to dry in the sun. Subtle fruity notes and very little bitterness make these beans popular with mid-range brands and craft chocolate makers. Fruition Chocolate, Rogue Chocolatier, and Manufaktura Czekolady all make artisan bars using Hispaniola beans.

POWER TO THE PEOPLE

Growers' unions and co-operatives have been vital to the development of cacao-growing in the region. Grupo CONACADO is an influential union made up of over 150 growers' associations – its members invented the Hispaniola fermentation method during a downturn in cocoa prices in the 1980s.

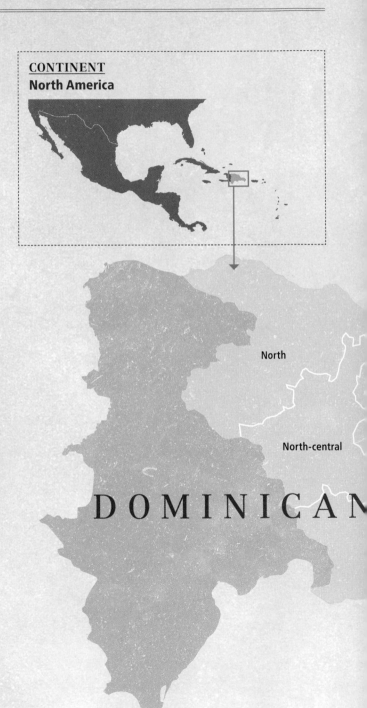

CONTINENT
North America

North

North-central

D O M I N I C A N

FACING THE ATLANTIC
Cacao trees grow across the east of the island facing the
Atlantic, where there are around 150,000 hectares (375,000
acres) of fertile land that is dedicated to cacao-farming.

GROWING REGION
The northeast region produces
the largest volumes of cocoa in the
country; it is also the region most
vulnerable to hurricanes and flooding,
making farming challenging

Northeast

Central

REPUBLIC

East

CAPITAL
Santo Domingo

GROWING REGION
Of the five agricultural regions
for growing cacao and coffee
(North, North-central, Northeast,
Central, and East), the East has
the most fertile soil

ENVIRONS
Cacao **grows** in the **shade** of **citrus**, banana,
and **avocado** trees

THE COUNTRY'S **PRODUCTION** IS LARGELY **ORGANIC** AND **FAIRTRADE** – HIGH-QUALITY COCOA FETCHES CONSISTENTLY **HIGH PRICES**

HARVEST
Months of cacao harvest

J	F	M	A	M	J	J	A	S	O	N	D

■ main crop   ■ mid crop

FAMILY **SMALLHOLDINGS** DOMINATE PRODUCTION, BUT THERE IS **A TREND** TOWARDS **LARGER FARMS**, PARTICULARLY IN THE **NORTHEAST REGION** OF THE COUNTRY

STAR VARIETY
Trinitario

FLAVOUR NOTES
Very slightly **acidic**,
with **yellow fruit**
flavours

A **LEADING EXPORTER** OF BOTH HIGH- AND **LOW-GRADE COCOA**

PRODUCTION
65,320 TONNES per year
1.4% of **WORLD PRODUCTION**

GRENADA

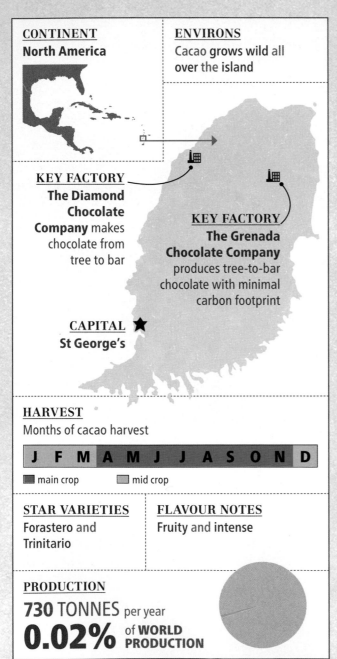

CONTINENT
North America

ENVIRONS
Cacao grows wild all over the island

KEY FACTORY
The Diamond Chocolate Company makes chocolate from tree to bar

KEY FACTORY
The Grenada Chocolate Company produces tree-to-bar chocolate with minimal carbon footprint

CAPITAL ★
St George's

HARVEST
Months of cacao harvest

| J | F | M | A | M | J | J | A | S | O | N | D |

■ main crop   ■ mid crop

STAR VARIETIES
Forastero and Trinitario

FLAVOUR NOTES
Fruity and intense

PRODUCTION
730 TONNES per year
0.02% of **WORLD PRODUCTION**

This small island is known for its fruity cocoa and one little company that inspired a chocolate revolution. Thanks largely to the work of one man, Grenada has become a symbol for ethical chocolate.

Like the other cacao-growing nations of the Caribbean, the crop was first successfully introduced to Grenada by the French in the late 1600s. More recently, Grenada has developed a reputation for high-grade cocoa, which is grown all over the island and processed locally.

GOING GREEN

When the American Mott Green moved to the island in the late 1980s, farmers were neglecting cacao in favour of spices such as cinnamon, cloves, and ginger. Green saw potential in growing and processing cocoa locally, and founded The Grenada Chocolate Company in 1999. He recruited friends and locals to help him build a tiny, solar-powered chocolate factory, and went into partnership with nearby farmers to process their beans. The factory is air-conditioned to prevent the chocolate bars from melting in the tropical heat, and the company transports the bars across the world via sailing boats and bicycles. Green sadly passed away in 2013, but the company has become a model for ethical, sustainable, tree-to-bar chocolate-making around the world.

TRAMPING THE BEANS

Grenadian cocoa beans are still dried just as they were 300 years ago. After fermenting, the producers spread out the beans on wooden platforms to dry in the sun. Workers then "tramp" through them, using their feet to shift the beans to ensure that they are dried evenly, and to pick out defective beans.

SAINT LUCIA

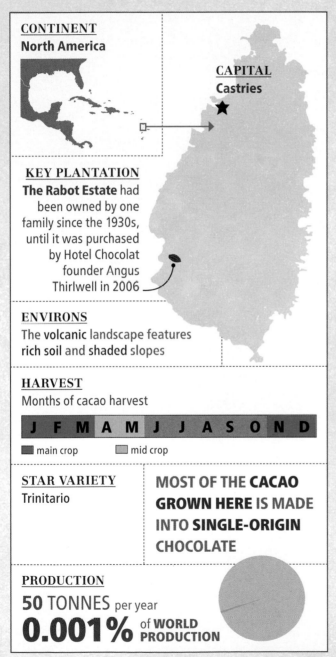

CONTINENT
North America

CAPITAL
Castries

KEY PLANTATION
The Rabot Estate had been owned by one family since the 1930s, until it was purchased by Hotel Chocolat founder Angus Thirlwell in 2006

ENVIRONS
The **volcanic** landscape features rich **soil** and **shaded** slopes

HARVEST
Months of cacao harvest

| J | F | M | A | M | J | J | A | S | O | N | D |

■ main crop   ■ mid crop

STAR VARIETY
Trinitario

MOST OF THE **CACAO GROWN HERE** IS MADE INTO **SINGLE-ORIGIN** CHOCOLATE

PRODUCTION
50 TONNES per year
0.001% of **WORLD PRODUCTION**

Associated with cacao-growing since the 18th century, Saint Lucia is undergoing a cocoa revival, partly thanks to one famous British chocolate company.

Cocoa has always been important to Saint Lucia, but until recently the industry lacked investment, with tourism taking precedence. Cocoa beans grown on the island were more likely to end up in low-grade, mixed-origin chocolate products than in high-end, traceable bars and chocolates.

REVIVING A PLANTATION

Inspired by a book on the history of cacao-growing in the Caribbean, Hotel Chocolat founder Angus Thirlwell purchased the Rabot Estate in 2006. The 57-hectare (140-acre) estate is one of the oldest on the island and had been owned by one family since the 1930s, but had become run-down and overgrown.

A REVITALIZED COCOA TRADE

Today, the majority of Saint Lucian cocoa is made into single-origin chocolate bars by Hotel Chocolat. The company has revived the estate, introducing new cacao-growing initiatives and opening a luxury hotel where visitors can experience the chocolate-making process for themselves. The land is now divided into 16 "côtes", or growing areas, each of which is said to have a distinct terroir. The company processes locally grown beans on the estate before shipping them back to Europe.

TRINIDAD AND TOBAGO

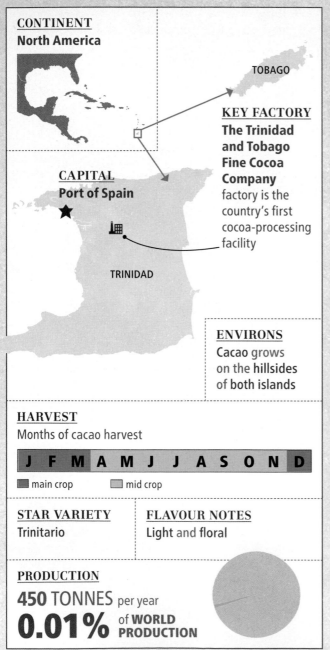

CONTINENT
North America

TOBAGO

KEY FACTORY
The Trinidad and Tobago Fine Cocoa Company factory is the country's first cocoa-processing facility

CAPITAL
Port of Spain

TRINIDAD

ENVIRONS
Cacao grows on the hillsides of both islands

HARVEST
Months of cacao harvest

J	F	M	A	M	J	J	A	S	O	N	D

■ main crop   ■ mid crop

STAR VARIETY
Trinitario

FLAVOUR NOTES
Light and floral

PRODUCTION
450 TONNES per year
0.01% of WORLD PRODUCTION

The islands of Trinidad and Tobago once formed one of the biggest cacao-growing nations on the planet, but trade dwindled in the 20th century. More recently, the islands have become a centre for cacao research, and a new factory has opened, seeking to revive cocoa production.

Trinidad and Tobago's relationship with cocoa dates back to 1525, when the Spanish first introduced the Criollo variety from Central America. These trees later cross-bred with the Forastero variety to produce a new hybrid cacao, named "Trinitario", after Trinidad.

Trinitario trees produce beans with some of the flavour characteristics of Criollo beans combined with the higher yields of Forastero trees. The success of the hybrid helped Trinidad and Tobago become a major player in the cocoa trade – at their peak, the islands were the third-largest cocoa producer in the world. By the 1920s, however, the spread of Witches' Broom disease and the global economic downturn had resulted in a dramatic reduction in output.

RESEARCH AND REGENERATION

It was in this difficult climate that the first cacao-research groups were formed, to help combat diseases and identify and develop disease-resistant varieties. The Cocoa Research Centre and International Genebank now house 2,400 varieties of cacao, representing about 80 per cent of the world's cacao.

In 2015, the Trinidad and Tobago Fine Cocoa Company was founded, with the aim of increasing the global visibility of Trinidadian cocoa and providing better prices for local farmers. The factory can process up to 150 tonnes of locally grown cacao per year.

CUBA

Better known as a producer of tobacco, sugar, and coffee, Cuba has also grown cacao for more than 200 years. Most cacao farms are found at the easternmost tip of the country, where the land juts out into the Atlantic Ocean.

Cacao was probably first brought to the island by the Spanish in around 1540, but didn't become a key crop until the late 18th century, with the arrival of the French from neighbouring Haiti. By 1827, there were 60 cacao plantations on the island, and Cuban cocoa production more than quadrupled over the next 70 years. Hot chocolate became a staple breakfast drink.

GUEVARA'S CHOCOLATE LEGACY

Today, 75 per cent of Cuba's cacao is grown in the east, in the hills surrounding Baracoa. Rainfall exceeds 230cm (90in) per year, creating humid conditions that are perfect for growing cacao. *Campesinos* (farmers) struggle to make enough money from cacao alone, so interplant it with other, more lucrative crops such as bananas.

Cocoa beans are sold to chocolate companies in Europe or the US, or processed locally, at the Ruben David Suarez Abella Complex in Baracoa. Ernesto "Che" Guevara founded the factory in the early 1960s, when he was Cuba's Minister of Industry. The factory still makes chocolate products using the original equipment, imported from what was then East Germany.

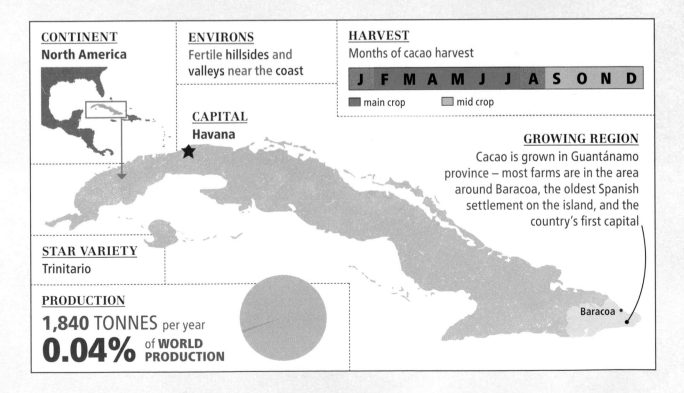

CONTINENT
North America

ENVIRONS
Fertile hillsides and valleys near the coast

HARVEST
Months of cacao harvest

| J | F | M | A | M | J | J | A | S | O | N | D |

■ main crop   ■ mid crop

CAPITAL
Havana

GROWING REGION
Cacao is grown in Guantánamo province – most farms are in the area around Baracoa, the oldest Spanish settlement on the island, and the country's first capital

Baracoa •

STAR VARIETY
Trinitario

PRODUCTION
1,840 TONNES per year
0.04% of WORLD PRODUCTION

ECUADOR

The eighth-largest producer in the world, Ecuador is a key source of fine-flavoured cocoa beans. The indigenous Arriba Nacional variety is highly regarded for its subtle fruity and floral flavours, but it faces competition from higher-yielding hybrids.

Despite producing just 5 per cent of the world's total cacao crop, Ecuador's output has increased dramatically in the last 15 years. Around 70 per cent of the fine-flavoured beans used in high-end, single-origin chocolate originate in Ecuador.

CACAO VARIETIES

The native Arriba Nacional cacao is genetically a Forastero variety but is noted for its fine flavour. Ecuadorian Arriba Nacional chocolate can be earthy and rich, and is often highlighted by subtle notes of orange blossom, jasmine, and spices.

In recent years, controversy has surrounded the introduction of CCN-51, a man-made hybrid cacao that produces larger yields at the expense of flavour. Although it is an attractive option for farmers, experts argue that Ecuador's genetic diversity and unique flavours are being lost.

FROM TREE TO BAR

Ecuador's cocoa industry is transforming itself. Instead of purely exporting beans, there's a move towards making chocolate as well. Making chocolate locally benefits the economy significantly more than simply exporting beans, and enables manufacturers to work directly with farmers. This simple tree-to-bar process is often used as a model for chocolate makers in other countries.

Companies such as Pacari and Montecristi are using local cacao to manufacture award-winning chocolate bars and couverture for export.

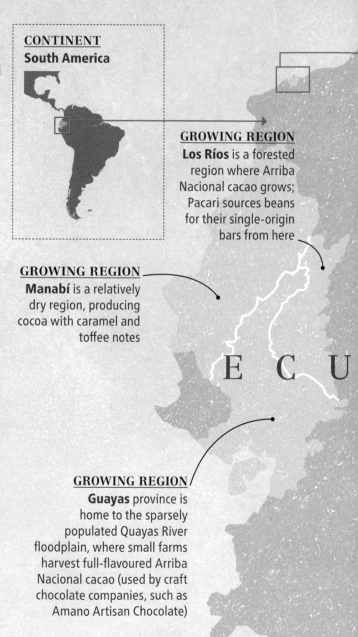

CONTINENT
South America

GROWING REGION
Los Ríos is a forested region where Arriba Nacional cacao grows; Pacari sources beans for their single-origin bars from here

GROWING REGION
Manabí is a relatively dry region, producing cocoa with caramel and toffee notes

GROWING REGION
Guayas province is home to the sparsely populated Quayas River floodplain, where small farms harvest full-flavoured Arriba Nacional cacao (used by craft chocolate companies, such as Amano Artisan Chocolate)

E C U

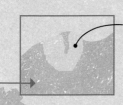

GROWING REGION
Esmereldas is a lush and fertile area and one of the poorest provinces in Ecuador – good-quality cocoa can fetch high prices and is transforming the lives of many farmers here

CAPITAL
Quito

KEY FACTORY
Montecristi Chocolate make fine, organic couverture from Arriba Nacional beans grown in Manabí

KEY FACTORY
Pacari Chocolate make single-origin, organic bars from local Arriba Nacional beans in their factory in southern Quito

A   D   O   R

LOCAL AND INTERNATIONAL MAKERS PRIZE NATIVE BEANS

ENVIRONS
Cacao crops grow on **fertile floodplains** that are **nourished by volcanic sediment**

LOCAL FACTORIES MAKE SINGLE-ORIGIN CHOCOLATE FROM INDIGENOUS CACAO

HARVEST
Months of cacao harvest

J	F	M	A	M	J	J	A	S	O	N	D

■ main crop   ■ mid crop

ECUADOR GROWS MORE FINE-FLAVOUR CACAO THAN ANY OTHER COUNTRY

STAR VARIETIES
Arriba Nacional and CCN-51

FLAVOUR NOTES
Highlights of **orange blossom, jasmine,** and **spices**

ARRIBA NACIONAL
Green or yellow with deep furrows, Arriba Nacional cacao is full of flavour.

TREE-TO-BAR CHOCOLATE-MAKING BENEFITS THE LOCAL ECONOMY

PRODUCTION
217,720 TONNES per year
5.6% of **WORLD PRODUCTION**

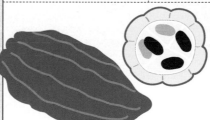

VENEZUELA

Producing some of the best-quality cocoa in the world, Venezuela is known for its local Criollo hybrids. Some of the delicately flavoured, pale-coloured varieties are highly prized by chocolate makers, in part because they are so difficult to source.

Venezuela was once one of the largest producers of cocoa in South America. Today, partly due to strict limits imposed by the government, its exports are a fraction of what they once were. The government's restrictions are intended to reduce the price of locally grown cocoa, making it accessible to the Venezuelan people, but the result is that often beans are left languishing in warehouses, unsold. While new chocolate factories continue to open, processing cocoa for the local market, very little of Venezuela's excellent cocoa is allowed to leave the country.

SEEKING RARE VARIETIES

The Porcelana variety of cacao grown in the west of the country produces pale, porcelain-like beans with delicately fruity and floral flavour notes. European chocolate makers prize these beans as some of the best in the world.

Equally prized are beans from the isolated village of Chuao on the northern coast, where cacao has been growing for over 400 years. While not technically a distinct cacao variety, a unique combination of genetics and terroir gives Chuao beans a balanced flavour with red-fruit notes and a hint of acidity. The difficulty in sourcing these beans – due to the export restrictions and the isolation of the plantation – means that Chuao cocoa commands high prices. In the hands of a skilled chocolate maker, it can be made into some of the best chocolate in the world.

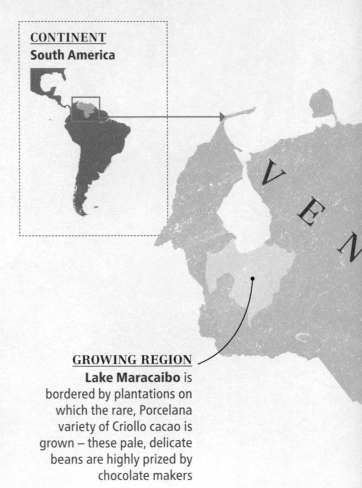

CONTINENT
South America

GROWING REGION
Lake Maracaibo is bordered by plantations on which the rare, Porcelana variety of Criollo cacao is grown – these pale, delicate beans are highly prized by chocolate makers

LEGISLATION AIMS TO KEEP COCOA CHEAP FOR LOCAL MAKERS

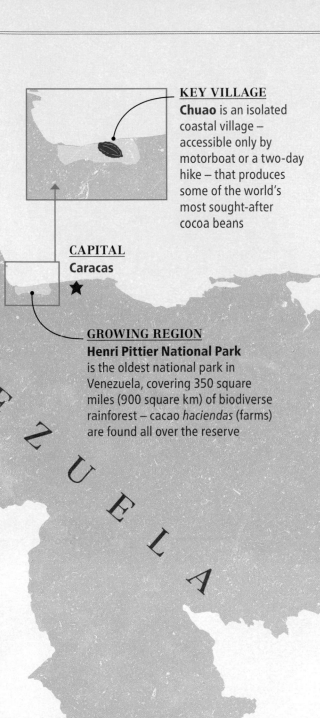

KEY VILLAGE
Chuao is an isolated coastal village – accessible only by motorboat or a two-day hike – that produces some of the world's most sought-after cocoa beans

CAPITAL
Caracas

GROWING REGION
Henri Pittier National Park is the oldest national park in Venezuela, covering 350 square miles (900 square km) of biodiverse rainforest – cacao *haciendas* (farms) are found all over the reserve

ENVIRONS
Cacao trees grow in **cloud forest** close to the **Caribbean Sea**

HARVEST
Months of cacao harvest

J	F	M	A	M	J	J	A	S	O	N	D

■ main crop   ■ mid crop

THE CHUAO PLANTATION IS **OWNED** BY THE **LOCAL COMMUNITY** AND MANAGED BY A **CO-OPERATIVE**

PORCELANA POD
Thought to be the most sought-after variety in the world, Porcelana is a sub-variety of Criollo cacao.

The smooth, rounded pods are very pale in colour

STAR VARIETIES
Porcelana and Criollo

FLAVOUR NOTES
Fruity and floral flavour notes

PRODUCTION
18,140 TONNES per year
0.4% of **WORLD PRODUCTION**

BRAZIL

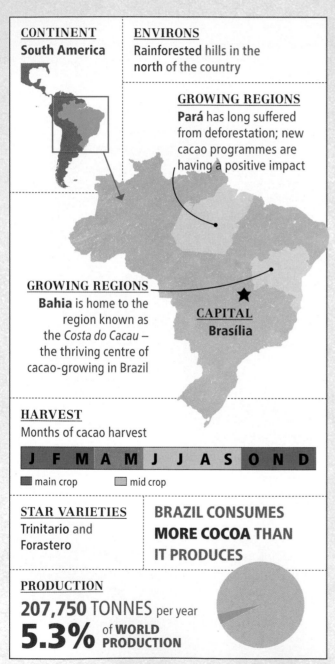

CONTINENT
South America

ENVIRONS
Rainforested hills in the north of the country

GROWING REGIONS
Pará has long suffered from deforestation; new cacao programmes are having a positive impact

GROWING REGIONS
Bahia is home to the region known as the *Costa do Cacau* – the thriving centre of cacao-growing in Brazil

CAPITAL
Brasília

HARVEST
Months of cacao harvest

J	F	M	A	M	J	J	A	S	O	N	D

■ main crop   ▢ mid crop

STAR VARIETIES
Trinitario and Forastero

BRAZIL CONSUMES MORE COCOA THAN IT PRODUCES

PRODUCTION
207,750 TONNES per year
5.3% of WORLD PRODUCTION

The largest country in South America, Brazil was once a powerhouse of cocoa production. Disease and economic factors have taken their toll on the industry, but there are signs of recovery.

Brazil was once the biggest cocoa producer in the Americas, but the industry has been decimated by disease. Decreased production combined with an increased local appetite for chocolate means that since 1998, Brazil has been a net importer of cocoa products.

DEVASTATED BY DISEASE

In 1989, Witches' Broom Disease hit Bahia, the most productive of Brazil's cacao-growing regions. The disease causes dense growths that look like a witch's broom – hence the name – and dramatically reduces the productivity of infected trees. Over the next decade, Witches' Broom destroyed much of Brazil's cacao crop, cutting output by 75 per cent. Today, many of the trees in Bahia have been replaced with more resilient varieties and there are some signs of recovery, but progress is slow.

REBUILDING THE COCOA INDUSTRY

Despite these problems, Brazil is still one of the top 10 cocoa producers in the world, and efforts are being made to increase production. Large multinational confectionery companies, such as Mars and Cargill, have initiated programmes to provide economic, social, and technical assistance to Brazilian cocoa farmers.

On a smaller scale, some farms are focusing on producing high-quality cocoa beans in order to increase financial returns. Growers at Fazenda Camboa, a cacao farm on the Costa do Cacau (Cocoa Coast) in southern Bahia, produce cocoa for craft chocolate makers.

COLOMBIA

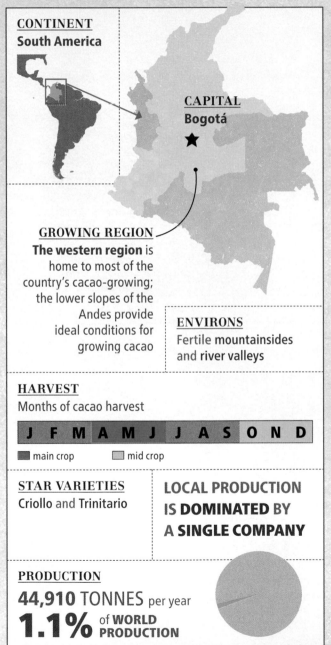

CONTINENT
South America

CAPITAL
Bogotá
★

GROWING REGION
The western region is
home to most of the
country's cacao-growing;
the lower slopes of the
Andes provide
ideal conditions for
growing cacao

ENVIRONS
Fertile **mountainsides**
and **river valleys**

HARVEST
Months of cacao harvest

J	F	M	A	M	J	J	A	S	O	N	D

■ main crop   ■ mid crop

STAR VARIETIES
Criollo and Trinitario

**LOCAL PRODUCTION
IS DOMINATED BY
A SINGLE COMPANY**

PRODUCTION
44,910 TONNES per year
1.1% of **WORLD
PRODUCTION**

**Focusing on quality as well as quantity,
Colombia is one of the world's biggest
exporters of fine-flavoured cocoa. Local
cacao varieties produce distinctive
chocolate featuring fruit or floral flavours.**

Colombia currently produces around one per
cent of the world's cocoa, but the government
has big ambitions for increasing production.
Unlike many countries, where increasing yields
are the driving economic force, initiatives in
Colombia are putting the emphasis on quality.

A REPUTATION FOR FINE COCOA

The Colombian government have focused their
attention on developing the fine-flavoured
varieties that the country is famous for, rather
than turning to higher-yield, bulk varieties.
There are plans to double production in the
coming years, including a government-backed
scheme to revitalize and replant 80,000
hectares (197,680 acres) of cacao-growing land.

By far the largest producer and exporter
of cocoa beans and chocolate products is the
family-owned company Casa Luker, which
purchases around one-third of the country's
crop. The company works directly with farmers
around Colombia, encouraging them to cultivate
local cacao varieties. The resulting cocoa beans
are turned into a range of chocolate products at
the Luker factory in Bogotá.

DIVERSE LOCAL FLAVOURS

Colombian chocolate is as varied as the regions
it comes from, but it often features subtle fruit
and floral flavour notes with hints of spice.
Colombia-based chocolate makers Cacao
Hunters seek out the very best beans from
across the country, and create bars to showcase
the diverse flavours of Colombian cocoa.

PERU

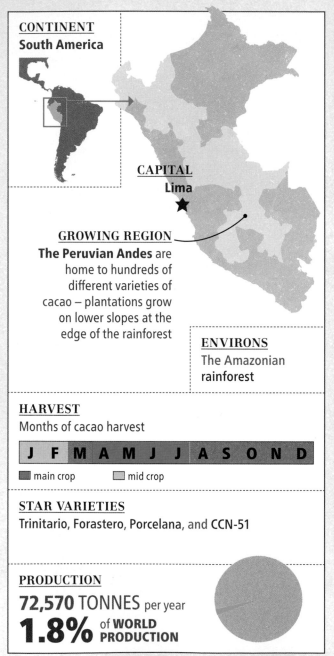

CONTINENT
South America

CAPITAL
Lima
★

GROWING REGION
The Peruvian Andes are
home to hundreds of
different varieties of
cacao – plantations grow
on lower slopes at the
edge of the rainforest

ENVIRONS
The Amazonian
rainforest

HARVEST
Months of cacao harvest

J	F	M	A	M	J	J	A	S	O	N	D

■ main crop   ■ mid crop

STAR VARIETIES
Trinitario, Forastero, Porcelana, and CCN-51

PRODUCTION
72,570 TONNES per year
1.8% of WORLD PRODUCTION

One of the largest and most well-known sources of fine-flavoured cocoa for the craft chocolate market, Peru's output is increasing rapidly. However, pressure to switch to high-yielding cacao varieties may damage Peru's reputation for flavour.

Since the 19th century, Peru has been one of South America's largest cocoa producers. In recent years, Peruvian cocoa has gained a reputation for its fine flavours, contributing to the rapid growth of national cocoa production.

TRACING CACAO ORIGINS

As well as cultivated cacao, numerous hybrid varieties can be found growing wild in the Amazonian rainforest. In the early 2000s, a team of researchers from Peru and the US discovered three new varieties of cacao, as well as finding specimens of the renowned Arriba Nacional variety, previously thought to be unique to Ecuador. Such research helps preserve hybrid varieties with ancient origins. Experts can then use these trees to propagate young plants, or to invent new, fine-flavoured varieties.

As in Ecuador, the increased popularity of the man-made cacao variety CCN-51 is causing controversy. Farmers plant it in place of native varieties in an effort to increase yields. Many fear that its spread could result in the loss of Peru's unique genetic diversity.

HAVEN FOR CRAFT COCOA

Peru's reputation as one of the original and most diverse sources of cocoa appeals to craft chocolate makers across the world. Fruition Chocolate, Original Beans, and Willie's Cacao all make chocolate bars that celebrate the unique flavours of Peru's heritage cocoa.

BOLIVIA

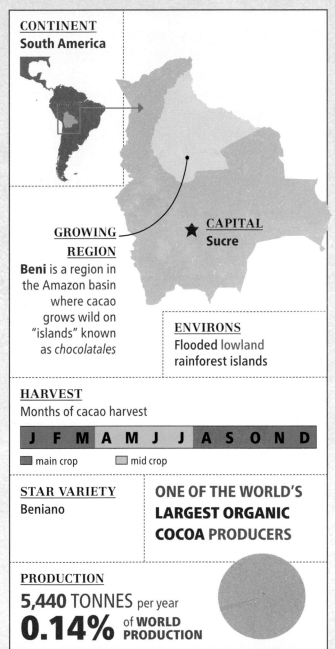

CONTINENT
South America

GROWING REGION
Beni is a region in the Amazon basin where cacao grows wild on "islands" known as *chocolatales*

CAPITAL
Sucre

ENVIRONS
Flooded lowland rainforest islands

HARVEST
Months of cacao harvest

J	F	M	A	M	J	J	A	S	O	N	D

■ main crop   □ mid crop

STAR VARIETY
Beniano

ONE OF THE WORLD'S LARGEST ORGANIC COCOA PRODUCERS

PRODUCTION
5,440 TONNES per year
0.14% of **WORLD PRODUCTION**

Known for the richly flavoured beans that grow wild in the northeastern province of Beni, Bolivia is seen by many as a model for sustainable, organic cocoa production.

Bolivia produces only around 5,440 tonnes of cocoa a year, yet it is one of the world's largest exporters of organic beans and has become famous for its wild cacao harvest.

WILD AMAZONIAN CACAO

Most chocolate in the world is made from cacao varieties that have been farmed by humans for hundreds of years. Bolivia's most famous cacao variety still grows wild and uncultivated on small patches of land in Beni, in the northeast of the country. The land floods so regularly that these outcrops are called *chocolatales*, or chocolate islands, and can be reached only by boat.

The German agriculturalist Volker Lehmann spotted the potential of this wild cacao, and invested in developing the infrastructure to enable traders to sell the cocoa for export. The full-flavoured beans now attract a significant premium, and local people are benefitting from the increase in international interest. Sustainable chocolate company Original Beans makes single-origin chocolate bars from Beniano cocoa.

WORKING TOGETHER

One key factor behind the success of Bolivian cacao is the organization of farmers and co-operatives. Founded in 1977, El Ceibo is a federation of several co-operatives that represents over 1,200 farmers in Bolivia. Working together, they provide training, support, and a single marketplace for their beans. El Ceibo also produces its own range of chocolate products that are sold internationally.

HONDURAS

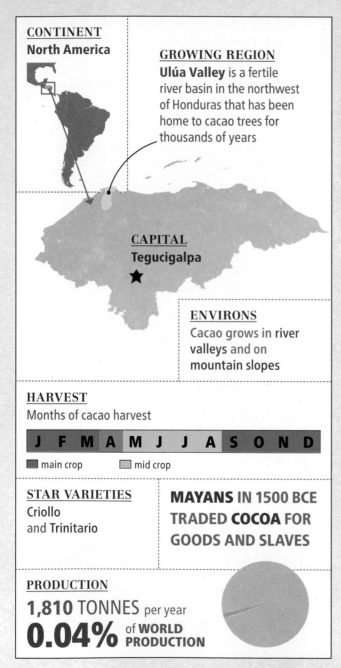

CONTINENT
North America

GROWING REGION
Ulúa Valley is a fertile river basin in the northwest of Honduras that has been home to cacao trees for thousands of years

CAPITAL
Tegucigalpa

ENVIRONS
Cacao grows in **river valleys** and on **mountain slopes**

HARVEST
Months of cacao harvest

J F M A M J J A S O N D

■ main crop   ■ mid crop

STAR VARIETIES
Criollo
and Trinitario

MAYANS IN 1500 BCE TRADED **COCOA** FOR GOODS AND SLAVES

PRODUCTION
1,810 TONNES per year
0.04% of **WORLD PRODUCTION**

Honduras has some of the earliest evidence of domesticated cacao cultivation in the world. The recent revival of some of these ancient local varieties may be the key to the country's future growth.

In the late 1990s, archaeologists discovered evidence of cocoa consumption in Honduras dating back to 1150 BCE. Traces of cocoa were found on shards of the region's famous ancient pottery, indicating that people had made cacao pulp or beans into drinks.

REGENERATING ANCIENT CACAO

Despite Honduras's historic link to cacao, many indigenous varieties were on the verge of extinction in the late 20th century due to a combination of economic factors, disease, and hurricane damage.

In 2008, Swiss company Chocolats Halba partnered with the Cacao Growers Association of Honduras (APROCACAHO) to reinvigorate the devastated Honduran cocoa trade in the wake of Hurricane Mitch. The company supports cacao farmers and pays fair prices for cocoa beans, as well as encouraging farmers to interplant cacao with hardwood trees, thereby helping reforestation in the countryside.

Research centres and companies such as Xoco Fine Cocoa are helping regenerate rare varieties of Honduran cacao. Xoco seeks out and analyses the very best cacao trees across the country, before selecting the finest specimens to reproduce and replant. When these cacao trees mature, they produce cocoa that has become highly prized in the craft chocolate industry – Xoco sells these rare beans to makers all over the world.

NICARAGUA

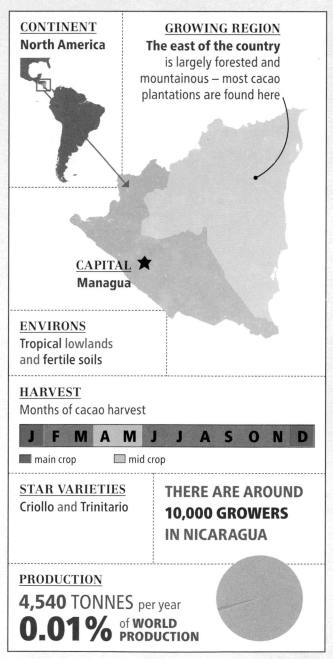

CONTINENT
North America

GROWING REGION
The east of the country is largely forested and mountainous – most cacao plantations are found here

CAPITAL ★
Managua

ENVIRONS
Tropical lowlands and fertile soils

HARVEST
Months of cacao harvest

| J | F | M | A | M | J | J | A | S | O | N | D |

■ main crop   ■ mid crop

STAR VARIETIES
Criollo and Trinitario

THERE ARE AROUND 10,000 GROWERS IN NICARAGUA

PRODUCTION
4,540 TONNES per year
0.01% of **WORLD PRODUCTION**

A relative newcomer to the cocoa industry, Nicaragua has gained a reputation for developing high-value, fine-flavoured cacao varieties.

In Nicaragua, farmers have tended to grow cacao as a second or third crop, rather than as a primary source of income. Most cocoa is used locally in traditional dishes and cocoa drinks.

REVOLUTION AND REGENERATION

In the 1980s, the Nicaraguan Revolution caused massive upheaval in the country. When the war ended in 1990, a series of programmes run by non-governmental organizations put agriculture at the heart of plans to reconstruct the country. Several schemes encouraged farmers to grow cacao, focusing on local, high-value Criollo varieties.

Today, programmes supplying cacao seedlings and education in growing, harvesting, and processing methods are gradually having a positive impact on the national economy. Experts believe that the country has almost 2 million hectares (5 million acres) of land suitable for cocoa production, though only a fraction of this potential is currently being realized.

QUALITY OVER QUANTITY

Despite producing limited quantities of cocoa, Nicaragua is renowned in the craft chocolate industry for its unique, fine-flavoured beans. Danish company Ingemann is one of the key players in cocoa research in the country: it has identified and developed six distinct sub-varieties of local cacao, supplying local farmers with around 350 million trees. Ingemann provides training and support, then buys back the resulting cocoa and exports it around the world.

MEXICO

Cacao has been cultivated in southern Mexico for over 2,000 years. Once one of the world's leading producers, the industry has suffered in recent years, but new initiatives aim to reverse the decline.

Many believe that Pre-Colombian civilizations first domesticated the cacao tree in the area now lying within southern Mexico. More than 2,000 years later, at the time of the Spanish Conquest, cacao plantations were common throughout southern Central America. Some of the largest plantations were in Soconusco and Tabasco – important growing areas to this day.

Although Mexico is often considered the home of cacao cultivation, production here has fallen dramatically since 2003, due to economic factors and pod disease. It is unusual for farmers to get a fair price for their cocoa, and therefore many have switched to other crops.

FRESH INITIATIVES

There are now several schemes to revive the industry in Mexico. One scheme, backed by the US confectionery company Hershey's, aims to provide training to farmers while introducing new disease-resistant cacao varieties.

There are signs of progress for cocoa farmers, but Mexico has a long road to recovery ahead, particularly as local demand for chocolate products is increasing and putting further pressure on production.

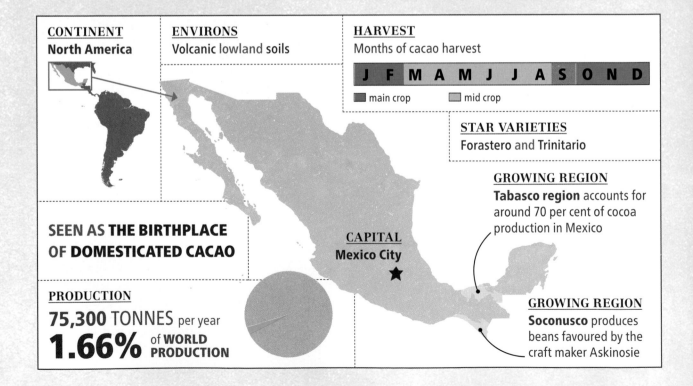

CONTINENT
North America

ENVIRONS
Volcanic lowland **soils**

HARVEST
Months of cacao harvest

| J | F | M | A | M | J | J | A | S | O | N | D |

■ main crop　　■ mid crop

STAR VARIETIES
Forastero and Trinitario

GROWING REGION
Tabasco region accounts for around 70 per cent of cocoa production in Mexico

SEEN AS THE BIRTHPLACE OF DOMESTICATED CACAO

CAPITAL
Mexico City
★

GROWING REGION
Soconusco produces beans favoured by the craft maker Askinosie

PRODUCTION
75,300 TONNES per year
1.66% of **WORLD PRODUCTION**

COSTA RICA

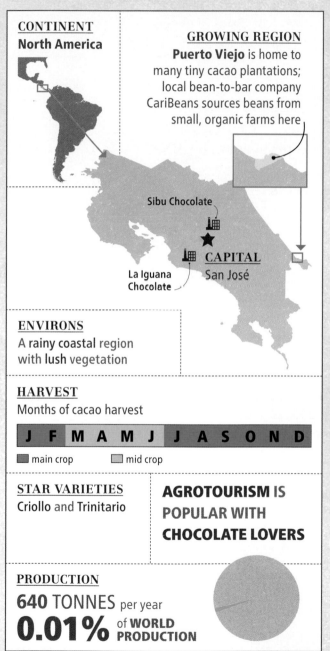

CONTINENT
North America

GROWING REGION
Puerto Viejo is home to many tiny cacao plantations; local bean-to-bar company CariBeans sources beans from small, organic farms here

Sibu Chocolate

CAPITAL
San José

La Iguana
Chocolate

ENVIRONS
A **rainy coastal** region with **lush** vegetation

HARVEST
Months of cacao harvest

J	F	M	A	M	J	J	A	S	O	N	D

■ main crop ■ mid crop

STAR VARIETIES
Criollo and Trinitario

AGROTOURISM IS POPULAR WITH CHOCOLATE LOVERS

PRODUCTION
640 TONNES per year
0.01% of **WORLD PRODUCTION**

With a deep historical connection to cocoa, Costa Rica has a focus on natural, sustainable production. Organic farms and agrotourism look to hold the key to the country's future success.

Costa Rica's location made it part of a key trade route for the Mayan civilization, and evidence suggests that chocolate was consumed by traders here in around 400 BCE. Despite this heritage, commercial cocoa production has never been a large contributor to the economy.

In the early 20th century, cacao was planted as a crop in Costa Rica by the United Fruit Company, replacing banana fields that had been destroyed by disease. These plantations still produce limited supplies of cocoa today.

CRAFT MAKERS

Costa Rican cocoa beans are popular with craft chocolate makers both locally and around the world. Costa Rican chocolate maker Sibu uses local cocoa and fresh ingredients in its highly respected range, sold internationally.

The primary cacao-growing area is Puerto Viejo on the Caribbean coast, but much of Costa Rica's cacao is grown on small family-run organic farms, such as La Iguana, located close to the Pacific west coast. La Iguana produces a range of chocolate products from cocoa powder to truffles and bars. They sell these products to subsidize income from the farm. Tourism is essential to farms like La Iguana. Volunteers can stay and work on the farm, helping with harvests and making chocolate.

This kind of agrotourism is becoming increasingly popular in Costa Rica, and may form the basis of a sustainable, "hands-on" chocolate industry for the future.

PANAMA

Cocoa accounts for just a tiny fraction of Panama's agricultural economy, but the country's connection to chocolate is a vital part of its tradition and heritage.

Panama's link to cocoa significantly predates the arrival of Europeans in Central America. Indigenous Kuna people have long used local cocoa to make a rich, sweet drink with impressive health benefits.

KUNA COCOA

The drink is prepared with hot water, spices, and cooked bananas for texture and sweetness. Recent scientific studies revealed that Kuna people who consume 4 or 5 cups of cocoa per day had one of the lowest incidences of heart disease and hypertension in the world, while those who stopped drinking the cocoa lost the associated benefits.

The research in Panama has provided a basis for several other studies that have highlighted the health benefits of flavanols found in cocoa.

COCOA TODAY

Despite producing relatively little cocoa for the international market, Panama is making the most of its natural resources and traditions with a growing agrotourism industry. The Bocas del Toro region in the north of the country produces most of Panama's exported cocoa, which is well regarded by international craft chocolate makers.

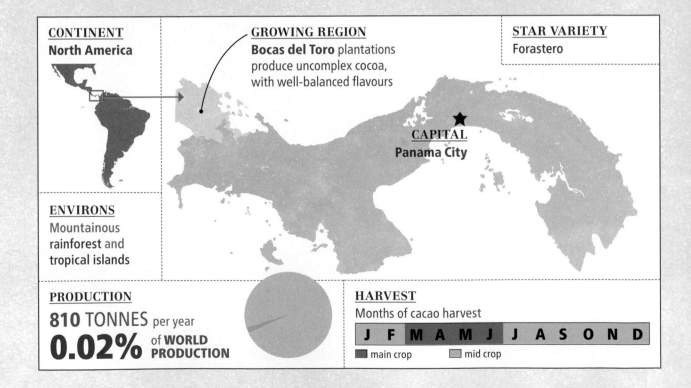

CONTINENT
North America

GROWING REGION
Bocas del Toro plantations produce uncomplex cocoa, with well-balanced flavours

STAR VARIETY
Forastero

CAPITAL
Panama City

ENVIRONS
Mountainous rainforest and tropical islands

PRODUCTION
810 TONNES per year
0.02% of **WORLD PRODUCTION**

HARVEST
Months of cacao harvest

J	F	M	A	M	J	J	A	S	O	N	D

■ main crop   ■ mid crop

HAWAII

Despite its remote location and limited cocoa production, Hawaii has a vibrant chocolate and cacao-growing industry. The entire annual crop is used by local makers.

Located in the middle of the Pacific, this group of islands forms the only US state where cacao can be grown. Its climate, location, and geographic conditions make growing and fermenting challenging, and gives cocoa variable flavour characteristics.

Cacao was introduced into Hawaii in 1850 by German botanist William Hillebrand, who planted the first trees in a botanical garden on the island of Oahu. It wasn't until the 1990s that commercial cacao farming was first explored.

PLANTATIONS IN DEMAND

Fewer than 80 hectares (200 acres) of land is used for growing cacao commercially. The Waialua Estate, run by food giant Dole, is the largest plantation. There are also smaller farms all over the islands, producing beans for a growing group of Hawaiian craft chocolate makers, including the tree-to-bar factory The Original Hawaiian Chocolate Factory (see pp64–65). Cocoa farmers struggle to meet increasing demand for fine-flavoured chocolate, forcing some makers to supplement local beans with imported ones.

Researchers believe that if the cocoa industry is developed further in Hawaii, it could add several million dollars to the state's economy.

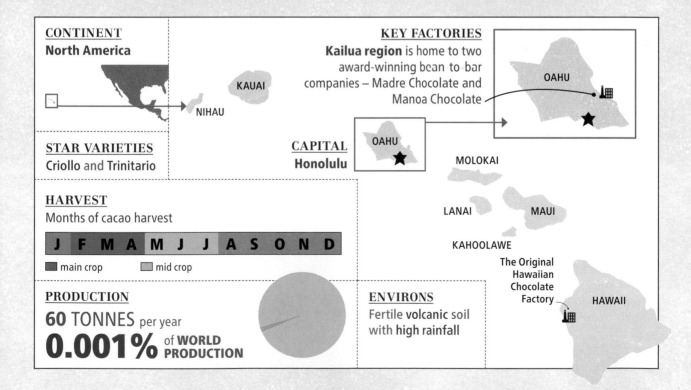

CONTINENT
North America

STAR VARIETIES
Criollo and Trinitario

HARVEST
Months of cacao harvest

J F M A M J J A S O N D

■ main crop   ■ mid crop

PRODUCTION
60 TONNES per year
0.001% of WORLD PRODUCTION

KEY FACTORIES
Kailua region is home to two award-winning bean-to-bar companies – Madre Chocolate and Manoa Chocolate

OAHU

CAPITAL
Honolulu

OAHU

KAUAI

NIHAU

MOLOKAI

LANAI   MAUI

KAHOOLAWE

The Original Hawaiian Chocolate Factory

HAWAII

ENVIRONS
Fertile **volcanic** soil with **high rainfall**

Behind the scenes | Kim Russell

THE FARMER

On the 6-hectare (15-acre) Crayfish Bay Estate in northwest Grenada, Kim Russell and local labourers grow and harvest organic cacao. Russell processes the fruit of the trees and prepares beans for local and international chocolate makers, as well as processing nibs to make traditional "cocoa rolls" that he sells on site.

Gives 90 per cent of earnings to local people

Also grows yam, banana, nutmeg, citrus fruits, and mango

When Kim Russell and his wife Lylette bought derelict buildings in northwest Grenada and cleared the land, they exposed the remains of a cacao plantation. Although Russell had no previous cacao-farming experience, he gained knowledge of farming, fermenting, and drying from local people in Grenada.

Russell has an unusual arrangement with workers on the farm. He has given control of running the estate – the growing, harvesting, hiring, and training – to local people in the community. In return for their stewardship, Russell gives them 90 per cent of what he earns from the wet cocoa grown on the land. He also shares other crops on the land, such as bananas, citrus fruits, yams, and mangoes with the local community. He believes this is a purer form of fair trade than the kind that involves payments to certification bodies. All practices are organic and no animals are kept for meat production on his land.

CHOCOLATE CHALLENGES

The constant maintenance of buildings, tools, and vehicles is challenging, along with the office work that comes with running a business. For Russell, however, the greatest challenge is to make enough money to keep moving forward. In countries such as Grenada, farmers cannot get a fair price for their cocoa and most require alternative sources of income. Labourers simply do not earn enough to cover basic needs, and as a result, young people are not interested in cacao-farming. The average age of a cocoa

farmer in Grenada today is 65, and it is difficult to foresee where the next generation of farmers will come from.

A DAY IN THE LIFE

The labouring and harvesting is undertaken by the local community, and Russell processes the beans. There are many daily tasks, including weighing wet cocoa, turning wet cocoa, opening and closing the drying drawers as the weather dictates, tramping, drying cocoa, and weighing and bagging dry cocoa. Russell also roasts, winnows, and produces nibs – sometimes grinding nibs to produce 100 per cent "cocoa rolls" that he sells locally.

MAKING COCOA ROLLS
Kim Russell grinds cocoa nibs to make a paste that he mixes with spices to make cocoa rolls. These rolls are mixed with milk, sugar, and water, and used to make cocoa tea.

TRAMPING
Russell undertakes the traditional process of tramping – farmers shuffle through the cocoa beans, turning them with their feet to ensure even drying.

COCOA BEAN VARIETIES
Different sub-varieties of cacao grow at the Crayfish Bay estate, each with different qualities. These two fermented varieties are notably different in colour and texture.

THE PLANTATION
Cacao is grown organically on the Crayfish Bay estate, in the shade of taller plants, such as banana and citrus fruit trees.

INDONESIA

The largest cocoa producer outside West Africa, Indonesia accounts for over 7 per cent of the world's cocoa. Cocoa is grown and processed across the vast archipelago, almost exclusively on small farms.

Indonesia is a large nation – comprising more than 17,000 islands – with a long history of growing cacao. Fine-flavoured Criollo varieties are thought to have been introduced to the country by the Spanish as early as 1560, but commercial cultivation didn't begin until the 20th century.

DIVERSE ORIGINS

Indonesia has the world's second-highest levels of biodiversity after Brazil. This, coupled with the sheer size of the country, means that growing conditions are varied. Up to 1.5 million hectares (2.5 million acres) of land is devoted to cocoa production, mostly on smallholder farms.

Around 75 per cent of production comes from the island of Sulawesi. Most Indonesian cocoa is used to make milk chocolate, but craft chocolate makers are celebrating the diverse local flavours with single-origin dark chocolate. International craft makers and fine chocolate companies source cocoa beans from across the archipelago, including Sumatra, Java, Bali, and Papua.

FUTURE CHALLENGES

Cocoa is one of Indonesia's most valuable exports, and output has grown rapidly in recent years. However, the future looks to be more challenging, with smallholders struggling to increase yields. Problems such as ageing trees, limited access to fertilizers, and poor farm maintenance hamper growth. The government is funding programmes to address these problems and help the country achieve its cocoa-producing potential, which is estimated to be around 1 million tonnes per year.

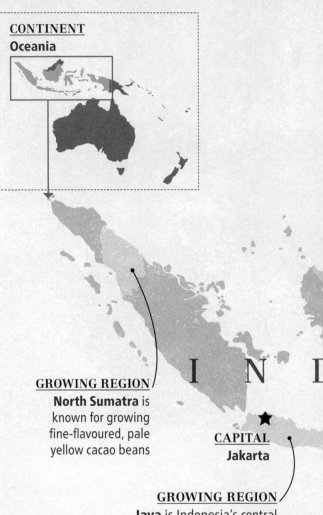

CONTINENT
Oceania

GROWING REGION
North Sumatra is known for growing fine-flavoured, pale yellow cacao beans

CAPITAL
Jakarta

GROWING REGION
Java is Indonesia's central island; Willie's Cacao and Chocolat Bonnat use caramel-flavoured beans grown in the volcanic soil of Surabaya, in East Java

MAKERS SOURCE BEANS FROM DIVERSE REGIONS

ENVIRONS
Terrains vary across the islands – **volcanic soil** and **humid rainforest** are common

INDONESIA IS THE **THIRD LARGEST PRODUCER** IN THE **WORLD**, BEHIND IVORY COAST AND GHANA

HARVEST
Months of cacao harvest

J	F	M	A	M	J	J	A	S	O	N	D

■ main crop   ■ mid crop

STAR VARIETIES
Trinitario and Forastero

FLAVOUR NOTES
Smoky flavours from beans **dried over flames**

GROWING REGION
Sulawesi produces about three-quarters of Indonesia's cocoa – mainly unfermented, low-grade varieties that are used for making cocoa butter and cocoa powder

MALAYSIA

GROWING REGION
Papua is the easternmost province of Indonesia, and the source of the rare, pale-coloured Belanda or Kerafat hybrid beans used by the sustainable company Original Beans

O N E S I A

TIMOR-LESTE

GROWING REGION
Bali's cocoa is used by Pipiltin Cocoa, a Jakarta-based chocolate company, and Åkesson's Organic

KEY PLANTATION
Sukrama farms, a small family estate, is the source of Trinitario beans used by Åkesson's Organic

IN **WET CONDITIONS**, COCOA **BEANS** ARE **DRIED** OVER **FIRES** MADE WITH **WOOD**, **COCONUT-SHELL**, OR **PROPANE**

PRODUCTION
290,300 TONNES per year
7.45% of **WORLD PRODUCTION**

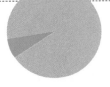

PHILIPPINES

One of the first countries in Asia to grow cacao, the Philippines soon developed a taste for it. Today, the traditional hot chocolate drink is more popular than ever.

Cacao was brought to the Philippines in the late 17th century by Spanish colonialists, who were eager to ensure a reliable supply of their favourite drink. Demand for chocolate is now so high that the country imports significantly more cocoa than it exports.

AZTEC-STYLE CHOCOLATE

The Philippine's favourite chocolate product has its roots in the earliest cocoa cultures of Central America: *tsokolate*, the local hot chocolate drink, is still made in a similar way to early Aztec cocoa drinks. Moulded discs of cocoa mass called *tablea* are combined with hot water and sugar, then whisked using a special utensil (see opposite) until the mixture reaches a smooth consistency. *Tsokolate* is traditionally served hot at breakfast. Modern versions of the drink are often diluted with milk and flavoured with ground peanuts. Much of the cocoa produced in the Philippines today is used to make *tablea* for the local market.

GROWTH IN CRAFT CHOCOLATE

Most Filipino cocoa intended for the international market is produced in bulk, but the country is fast becoming known for fine-flavoured cocoa.

American craft chocolate maker Shawn Askinosie works with farmers in the Davao region to produce award-winning chocolate bars. The success of this partnership has encouraged others to invest in cacao in the region. The family-run company Malagos Chocolate, based in Davao, makes internationally renowned chocolate, as well as running courses in sustainable cacao-farming.

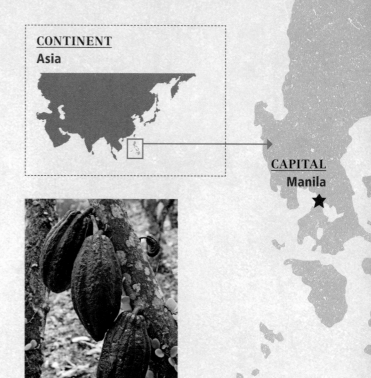

CONTINENT
Asia

CAPITAL
Manila

CACAO ON THE TREE
Trees grow on the forested slopes of the southern mountain ranges on the island of Mindanao. It takes 3–5 years for a cacao tree to produce fruit.

P H I L I

FILIPINOS LOVE AZTEC-STYLE HOT CHOCOLATE

GROWING REGION
Davao, a region on the island of Mindanao, has become well-known for cocoa grown close to the coast in the foothills of the Talomo Mountain Range

Davao City

P P I N E S

ENVIRONS
Conditions are **rainy** and **tropical** in the **foothills** of mountains

THE **ARCHIPELAGO** IS AN **IMPORTANT** SOURCE OF **COCOA PRODUCTS** FOR THE EMERGING CHOCOLATE INDUSTRY IN **SOUTHEAST ASIA**

HARVEST
Months of cacao harvest

J	F	M	A	M	J	J	A	S	O	N	D

■ main crop   ■ mid crop

STAR VARIETIES
Trinitario and **Forastero**

FLAVOUR NOTES
Subtle notes of **nutmeg** and **spice**

MOLINILLO WHISKS
Just as in Central America, hot chocolate is traditionally prepared using a wooden whisk called a *molinillo* or *batidor*.

THE PHILIPPINES **IMPORTS** AROUND **FIVE TIMES MORE** COCOA THAN IT **EXPORTS**

PRODUCTION
4,380 TONNES per year
0.1% of **WORLD PRODUCTION**

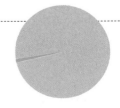

VIETNAM

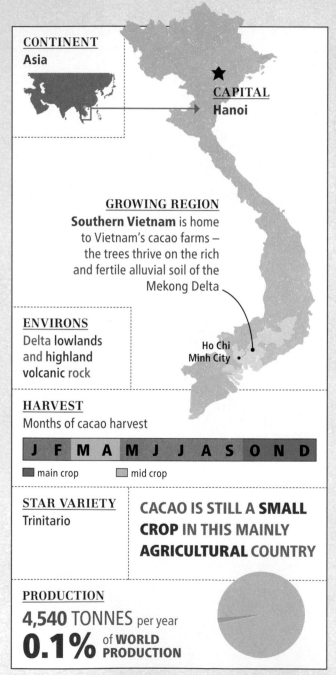

CONTINENT
Asia

CAPITAL
Hanoi

GROWING REGION
Southern Vietnam is home to Vietnam's cacao farms – the trees thrive on the rich and fertile alluvial soil of the Mekong Delta

Ho Chi
Minh City

ENVIRONS
Delta **lowlands** and **highland volcanic** rock

HARVEST
Months of cacao harvest

J	F	M	A	M	J	J	A	S	O	N	D

■ main crop   ■ mid crop

STAR VARIETY
Trinitario

CACAO IS STILL A SMALL CROP IN THIS MAINLY AGRICULTURAL COUNTRY

PRODUCTION
4,540 TONNES per year
0.1% of WORLD PRODUCTION

A relative newcomer to the world stage, Vietnam's cocoa industry is still small. However, thanks to the efforts of one local company, it is known for producing some of the best chocolate in the world.

Cacao was originally brought to Vietnam by the French in the late 1800s, but it wasn't until the Soviet Union endorsed the crop in the 1980s that cacao was planted on a large scale.

CHOCOLATE FOR THE EASTERN BLOC

By the time the cacao plantations had reached maturity in the 1990s, the Soviet Union was gone and new buyers had to be found. Large cocoa-processing companies came to the region, and cocoa began to be supplied to Indonesia and Malaysia for bulk-made chocolate products. More recently, the US-funded Success Alliance has become involved in the Vietnamese cocoa trade, training tens of thousands of smallholder farmers in sustainable cacao-growing methods.

A NEW FOCUS ON SUSTAINABILITY AND QUALITY

In 2011, two Frenchmen brought Vietnamese cocoa to the attention of the world's craft chocolate lovers. Samuel Maruta and Vincent Mourou met while travelling the country, and a visit to a cacao farm sparked the creation of Marou Chocolate. Marou makes chocolate in Ho Chi Minh City using cocoa beans sourced from the surrounding river delta. Single-estate bars celebrate the flavours of the key growing regions, including Ben Tre, Tien Giang, and Ba Ria.

PAPUA NEW GUINEA

The country of Papua New Guinea produces some of the world's most distinctive cocoa, with a complex fruity and smoky flavour.

Papua New Guinea was one of the world's largest cocoa producers, but insect infestations between 2008 and 2012 diminished the country's cacao plantations. Despite reduced output, the distinctive flavour of the fire-dried cocoa beans ensures popularity with craft chocolate makers.

STARTING FROM SCRATCH
Up to 80 per cent of farmers abandoned cacao during the insect infestation. Crops had been decimated by cocoa pod borers – a species of moth whose larvae feed on cacao beans. Subsequent investment from the government, cocoa production companies, and the World Bank enabled farmers to start again, planting hundreds of thousands of new seedlings.

FIRE-DRIED COCOA BEANS
The high humidity and rainfall in Papua New Guinea means that farmers cannot dry their cocoa beans in the sun, so beans are dried over wood fires instead. The still-damp cocoa beans absorb smoke particles from the warm air, taking on a barbecue-like flavour. Technically, the smoky flavour is a flaw in the cocoa, but some craft makers find it adds interest to their chocolate.

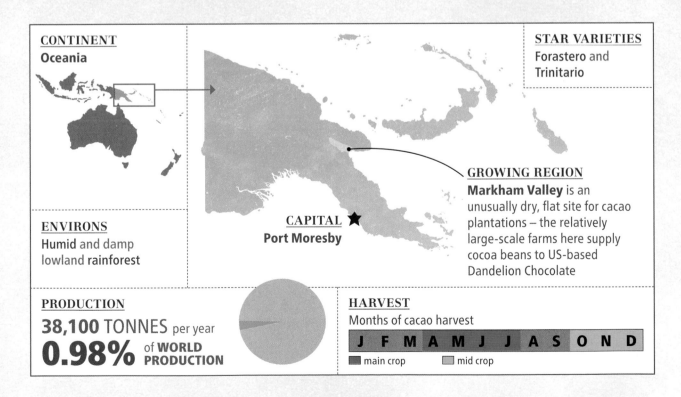

CONTINENT
Oceania

STAR VARIETIES
Forastero and Trinitario

ENVIRONS
Humid and damp lowland rainforest

CAPITAL
Port Moresby

GROWING REGION
Markham Valley is an unusually dry, flat site for cacao plantations – the relatively large-scale farms here supply cocoa beans to US-based Dandelion Chocolate

PRODUCTION
38,100 TONNES per year
0.98% of WORLD PRODUCTION

HARVEST
Months of cacao harvest

J	F	M	A	M	J	J	A	S	O	N	D

■ main crop   ■ mid crop

INDIA

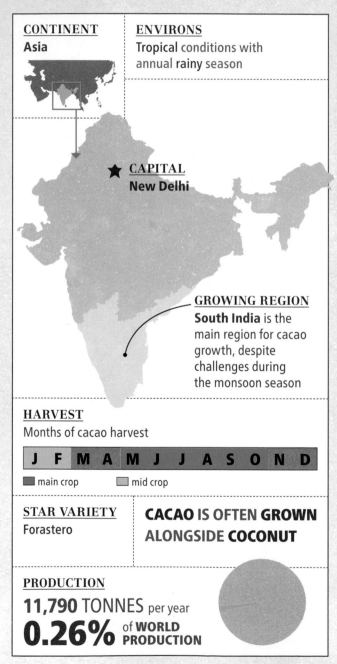

CONTINENT	ENVIRONS
Asia	Tropical conditions with annual rainy season

★ **CAPITAL**
New Delhi

GROWING REGION
South India is the main region for cacao growth, despite challenges during the monsoon season

HARVEST
Months of cacao harvest

J F M A M J J A S O N D

■ main crop   □ mid crop

STAR VARIETY
Forastero

CACAO IS OFTEN GROWN ALONGSIDE COCONUT

PRODUCTION
11,790 TONNES per year
0.26% of WORLD PRODUCTION

Producing less than one per cent of the world's cocoa at present, India has big plans for the future. Much of the country's current cocoa production is the result of research carried out by the British chocolate company, Cadbury.

Cacao was first cultivated in India in the 18th century, when the British established a few small plantations. Today, cacao plantations in the states of Andhra Pradesh, Tamil Nadu, Kerala, and Karnataka feed India's growing demand for chocolate.

COLONIAL COCOA

Indian cocoa has long been tied up with British involvement. Criollo varieties were grown on small farms run by the British trading company, the East India Company, producing chocolate for the colonial elite. It wasn't until the mid-20th century that Cadbury began research into growing the crop.

Established Criollo varieties were quickly replaced by higher-yielding Forastero varieties, and by the 1970s, cacao had become a commercial crop. Cadbury – owned today by Mondelez International – now runs Cocoa Life, a programme that supports around 100,000 cocoa farmers across the southern states.

CHOCOLATE FOR THE FUTURE

The bulk of Indian cocoa is used by large confectionery companies to make chocolate products for the Indian market. However, India's exports are increasing with global demand, and although very few high-end chocolate companies use beans from India, the Austrian bean-to-bar company Zotter produces single-origin chocolate with beans from Kerala.

AUSTRALIA

You may never have tasted chocolate made from Australian cocoa beans, but it's likely that you will do soon. With cocoa production doubling year on year, Australia is a rising star of the chocolate world.

At around 20 degrees south of the equator, Queensland is on the very edge of the global cacao-growing band. Until recently, cacao was not a commercial-scale crop, but there's now a small but flourishing industry.

BLOSSOMING INDUSTRY

Cacao has been grown in Australia for many years, but usually in the form of trials set up by local government or multinational confectionery companies. It's only in the last decade or so that the trial farms have become commercially viable plantations, and Far North Queensland is at the centre of this new movement.

GROWING LOCAL

Currently, all the cacao grown in Australia is made into products sold locally. Queensland-based Daintree Estates make chocolate bars, couverture, cocoa tea, and beauty products from beans grown on their own estate. Farmers grow cacao on small farms along the coast, and as company shareholders benefit from increasing sales. By keeping the focus at a local level, Daintree hopes to grow Australia's cocoa industry organically and sustainably.

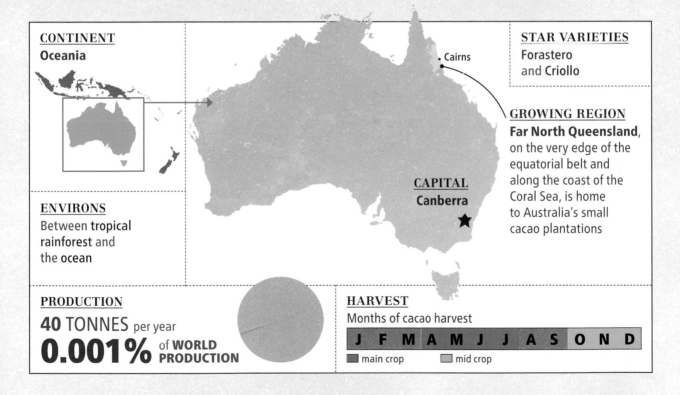

CONTINENT
Oceania

STAR VARIETIES
Forastero and **Criollo**

• Cairns

GROWING REGION
Far North Queensland, on the very edge of the equatorial belt and along the coast of the Coral Sea, is home to Australia's small cacao plantations

CAPITAL
Canberra

ENVIRONS
Between **tropical rainforest** and the **ocean**

PRODUCTION
40 TONNES per year
0.001% of **WORLD PRODUCTION**

HARVEST
Months of cacao harvest

J	F	M	A	M	J	J	A	S	O	N	D

■ main crop   ■ mid crop

CHOOSE

How do you choose chocolate? Find out how to pick out the finest varieties: decode the labels, unwrap the ingredients, and discover the signs of true quality.

THE REAL DEAL

There is now a wonderfully tempting array of chocolate to choose from. With so many packaging styles and chocolate types on offer, just how do you pick the cream of the crop? With the help of a little research into the producers and these indicators of quality, it is easy to choose good-quality chocolate that lasts well, is full of flavour, and is ethically produced.

CHOOSING BARS

Thanks to the explosive growth of bean-to-bar and fine chocolate on the market, it is now easier than ever to source delicious-tasting, good-quality chocolate. It can be difficult to know what to buy, as some producers use craft-style packaging and labelling, despite making chocolate that is anything but artisan. The easiest way to assess quality is to look at the chocolate and taste it before you buy (see pp124–29). It isn't possible to do this in many shops, so here are some other indicators that can inform your choice and help you to identify truly high-quality chocolate products.

THE LABEL

Make sure you examine the wording on the packaging. Ignore phrases such as "hand-made", which are meaningless – all chocolate is made by some mechanical processes involving machinery. Instead, look out for text describing the cocoa beans, or the bean-to-bar process.

The company name should be obvious. Opt for bean-to-bar chocolate makers who are open about how their chocolate is sourced and processed.

Cocoa percentages should be high. Keep in mind the usual ratios for each type of chocolate (see p103).

The origin of beans should be traceable. This is a sign that the maker is involved in sourcing the beans used in the chocolate.

Certification shows whether ingredients have been traded fairly (see pp52–55). Are they grown with minimal use of pesticides (see pp110–11)?

On the reverse there is a list of ingredients – does the chocolate contain artificial additives or palm oil (see p101)? As a general rule, the fewer ingredients, the better. Look out for information about the maker and how he or she operates.

The bean variety may be listed. If there is detailed information, this is an indication that the maker knows where the beans came from.

RESEARCH THE MAKER

It may not be the easiest task when you are in the shop, but there is no substitute for research into a chocolate maker. If a maker creates chocolate from bean to bar, the chances are that the company website and label will mention this. Search for reviews on blogs and food sites to help you decide if a particular chocolate is a good buy.

CHOOSING CHOCOLATES

Try to buy truffles, bonbons, and filled chocolates from a specialist chocolate shop. Shop assistants should be knowledgeable about the chocolatiers' ingredients and processes, so don't be afraid to ask. Find out where they source their ingredients from: most chocolatiers use ready-made couverture chocolate, rather than making the chocolate from scratch, so ask where they get it from and look into the maker.

When buying filled chocolates, ask about shelf life. The best chocolates are made with fresh ingredients and no preservatives, giving them a shelf life of 1–2 weeks.

MAKE SURE YOU CAN ASK ABOUT INGREDIENTS AND PROCESSES

Fine-quality chocolates are coated in glossy, perfectly tempered chocolate

Decorative flourishes should be perfectly finished

DEFECTS IN CHOCOLATES

Avoid chocolates with a dull, lacklustre finish or white patches on the surface. These are signs of bloom, caused by storing at the wrong temperature. Too hot, and cocoa butter in the chocolate melts and rises to the surface; too cold, and condensation draws sugar out of the chocolate. Pay attention to the colour of the chocolate. Dark chocolate should be a rich, deep brown in colour; darker hues indicate that the cocoa has been burnt.

Bloom on the surface of the chocolates indicates that they have been stored incorrectly

UNWRAPPING THE INGREDIENTS

Ingredients lists can be confusing, but it takes just two simple ingredients to make dark chocolate, and three ingredients to make milk chocolate. The different ways that makers choose and combine these ingredients make each chocolate bar unique.

COCOA BEANS

The key ingredient in any dark or milk chocolate and the biggest influence on flavour, cocoa beans are at the heart of all chocolate. Cocoa is grown all over the world, but the confectionery industry tends to use bulk-produced beans from West Africa. For finer-quality and craft chocolate, the beans can come from as far afield as Ecuador, Vietnam, or the Caribbean. Some countries, such as Madagascar, are reknowned for producing beans with a distinctive flavour profile.

On chocolate packaging, cocoa beans are referred to as cocoa mass, cocoa solids, or simply cocoa or cacao. They all refer to the same thing: ground and conched cocoa beans.

Cocoa beans from different countries or growing regions may look similar to one another, but their flavour can vary considerably

COCOA BEANS ARE AT THE HEART OF ALL CHOCOLATE

WHAT IS THE PERCENTAGE?
The percentage of "cocoa solids" you see on a chocolate label includes both the cocoa beans and any added cocoa butter. A dark chocolate labelled as "70% cocoa" may contain 65% cocoa beans and 5% added cocoa butter.

Craft chocolate makers seek out beans with a distinctive flavour profile, often working directly with farmers

COCOA BUTTER

A naturally occurring fat found inside the cocoa bean, cocoa butter is extracted from cocoa mass. Producers crush melted cocoa mass in a hydraulic press through a fine mesh. Most cocoa butter is then deodorized before use, although undeodorized butters retain more of the original flavour of the bean.

Many chocolate makers mix additional cocoa butter into their chocolate to improve its texture and make it easier to work with, although confectionery chocolate usually includes cheaper fats or oils instead (see box below). Cocoa butter is only essential in white chocolate, which is made without the solid part of the cocoa bean.

Cocoa butter is made in large blocks that have a waxy texture – most blocks retain almost none of the flavour of the original beans

Cocoa butter pellets are a favourite of chocolate makers and chocolatiers, as they melt much more quickly than blocks

PALM OIL VS COCOA BUTTER

In the confectionery industry, vegetable fats – usually palm oil – are often used in place of cocoa butter to make chocolate smoother. The addition of palm oil to confectionery is one of the biggest controversies in the chocolate world. Although significantly cheaper than cocoa butter, it is often considered to be environmentally destructive and has been linked to cardiovascular disease. In Europe, for example, chocolate that has had vegetable fats substituted for cocoa butter is not legally allowed to be called "chocolate", and is sold variously as "compound chocolate", "family chocolate" or simply "chocolate flavour coating".

SUGAR

Transforming the intense natural flavours of cocoa beans into the deliciously sweet confection, sugar is the second most important ingredient in chocolate. Dark chocolate usually contains 30–40 per cent sugar, and milk and white chocolate can contain 40 per cent or more. Most chocolate contains mild-tasting cane sugar, but alternative sweeteners, such as coconut palm sugar and lucuma powder, are becoming more popular.

Cane sugar is the sweetener in most craft chocolate bars – it's mild in flavour, and doesn't overwhelm the flavour profile of the chocolate

MILK POWDER

Sometimes referred to as "milk solids", milk powder is an essential ingredient of milk and white chocolate. Most chocolate is made with cow's milk, but goat's milk, sheep's milk, and even camel's milk chocolate is available, as well as vegan chocolate made with milk substitutes.

Milk powder adds creaminess and a little sweetness to milk and white chocolate

EXTRA INGREDIENTS
Chocolate may include other useful but non-essential ingredients.

Vanilla powder is often used as a flavouring in chocolate. Some makers add it to hide cheap or mouldy cocoa. It is not usually needed in dark chocolate, but is an important component of white.

Lecithin is an emulsifier extracted from soy beans or sunflower seeds. It binds sugar and cocoa particles with cocoa butter, making chocolate creamy and smooth.

THE RIGHT BLEND

Chocolate makers start with high-quality cocoa beans, and use them to make a single-origin chocolate. Some experiment by blending or adding extra ingredients and flavourings. Craft chocolate makers are also exploring an exciting trend for unconventional recipes.

CREATING A RECIPE

The success of any recipe begins with the right ingredients, and this rule extends to a bar of chocolate. Chocolate makers experiment with finding the perfect recipe to bring out the best flavour in their beans – by roasting at different temperatures, conching for varying periods of time, blending with other beans, or changing the ingredients' ratios.

Makers may achieve interesting flavour profiles by blending beans of different origin. Some makers take two or more beans with contrasting flavour profiles and combine them into a single chocolate that features characteristics of each bean. Blending beans well is an art, but some makers use blending to disguise flaws in poor-quality cocoa. It is for this reason that purists tend to favour single-origin dark chocolate, as it is a more accurate reflection of the flavour of the original bean.

It is an exciting time to be a craft chocolate maker. From creating milk chocolate without sugar, to using powdered fruit or ground insects in place of milk powder, chocolate makers are pushing gastronomic boundaries with new recipes.

The proportions

Different types of chocolate are made with different ratios of key ingredients. The classic ratios are below, and the following pages cover the wide spectrum of dark, milk, and white chocolate varieties.

70% cocoa

30% sugar

CLASSIC DARK
Dark chocolate is all about the cocoa beans, with sugar to sweeten it, and sometimes a little cocoa butter too.

25% milk powder

35% sugar

40% cocoa

CLASSIC MILK
Milk chocolate contains both sugar and milk powder to round off the more intense notes of the beans.

30% cocoa butter

30% milk powder

40% sugar

CLASSIC WHITE
White chocolate contains no cocoa beans, only cocoa butter, milk powder, and sugar. Vanilla is a common flavouring.

DARK CHOCOLATE SPECTRUM

With just two key ingredients – cocoa beans and sugar – dark chocolate is as simple as chocolate gets, yet it comes in an extraordinary array of varieties. Single-origin chocolate and carefully selected blends showcase the intense natural flavours of cocoa beans, undiluted.

PURE CHOCOLATE

Dark chocolate is a simple food with a remarkable flavour complexity. Good-quality bean-to-bar dark chocolate usually contains a high proportion of cocoa solids, to maximize the impact of the chocolate flavour. The absence of milk powder also helps to focus the flavour on the beans. However, without milk, which can balance imperfections and round off flavour, makers must refine and conche dark chocolate for longer than milk chocolate – even several days – to create the perfect flavour profile.

Many craft chocolate makers have developed relationships with particular growers to create characteristic single-origin varieties – the aim is to extract the best possible flavour and texture from their favourite beans. Other makers play with flavour, texture, and added ingredients.

UNADULTERATED FLAVOUR NOTES

If you're used to eating confectionery chocolate, you may find that dark chocolate is an acquired taste, but it is worth acclimatizing yourself to the deeper and more complex flavours in order to appreciate chocolate in its most pure form. Start with a relatively low cocoa percentage dark chocolate, or even a dark milk (see pp106–107) and gradually work your way up the scale.

100% cocoa

100% DARK

Made from cocoa beans with no added sugar or flavourings, 100 per cent chocolate promotes the ultimate flavour of the cocoa bean. Chocolate makers may add cocoa butter to cut through any bitterness and give a smoother mouthfeel.

SIGNS OF QUALITY

- **Pure chocolate** may taste a little bitter, but the cocoa hit shows off the full flavour profile of the cocoa beans.
- **Good-quality** dark chocolate has a rich, deep brown colour.

40–50%
sugar

30%
sugar

65% cocoa

60–70%
cocoa

30–40%
sugar

50–60%
cocoa

5%
flavourings

UNREFINED DARK

Unrefined chocolate is traditionally made with minimal processing in simple stone grinders. Rather than being conched to the smallest possible particle size, cocoa beans and sugar are coarsely ground in a traditional stone mill before being moulded into bars.

SIGNS OF QUALITY

• **Unrefined dark** chocolate has a crunchy, biscuit-like texture, and may crumble a little when broken.

FLAVOURED DARK

When flavouring dark chocolate, makers search for ingredients that match or complement the flavour of the bean itself. During the conching process, makers add flavourings, such as spices or freeze-dried fruit powders, into the chocolate.

SIGNS OF QUALITY

• **Flavourings** should be strong enough to be noticed while subtly complementing the natural flavour notes in the cocoa.

• **Craft chocolate makers** source flavours from across the globe, as well as celebrating ingredients from their local area.

ALTERNATIVE SUGAR DARK

In recent years, some makers have started to experiment with sweeteners other than cane sugar. Coconut palm sugar is a popular choice – it has a low glycemic index and its subtle, toasted coconut flavour works well with chocolate.

SIGNS OF QUALITY

• **Alternative sugars** should not affect the finished texture of the chocolate – it will still be smooth-textured and glossy.

MILK CHOCOLATE SPECTRUM

First created in 1875 by the Swiss chocolatier Daniel Peter, milk chocolate was an instant hit, thanks to its smooth flavour and long shelf life. Today, around 40 per cent of all chocolate consumed globally contains dairy. There is a wide spectrum of milk chocolate to choose from, and the variety is growing.

MILK MATTERS

For many, chocolate and milk are a match made in heaven. However, cocoa and moisture are not natural bedfellows – in order for the ingredients to combine perfectly, makers must condense milk and combine it with sugar and cocoa nibs to produce a "chocolate crumb" mixture that is eventually ground and conched into bars. Some makers add vanilla, to enhance flavour, and emulsifiers to bind the ingredients together. Most chocolate makers also add cocoa butter to make chocolate easy to work with, but cheaper confectionery often contains other vegetable fats.

The sugar levels in milk chocolate are not much higher than those in dark chocolate – the sweeter flavour is largely due to lactose, which is a natural sugar found in milk.

CRAFT MAKERS ARE REINVENTING MILK CHOCOLATE

Experimentation with milk chocolate is a major trend in the modern chocolate industry. Small craft chocolate makers enjoy pushing boundaries and redefining our expectations of milk chocolate. Some increase the cocoa content to make a dark milk, or experiment with different milks to suit individual tastes and dietary needs.

25–35% milk powder

25–35% sugar

25–35% cocoa

CLASSIC MILK

The proliferation of cheap confectionery chocolate has given milk chocolate negative connotations, but there is lots to like about a good-quality variety that marries smooth texture with rich flavour.

SIGNS OF QUALITY

- **Milk chocolate** should not include vegetable fats or artificial flavourings.
- **Good-quality** chocolate has a rich, red-brown colour and should "snap" when you break it.

50–70% cocoa

20–25% sugar

20–25% milk powder

30% cocoa

30% milk powder

5% flavouring

35% sugar

50–70% cocoa

20–25% sugar

20–25% unusual milk powder

DARK MILK

Somewhere between a classic milk and a dark chocolate, dark milk chocolate contains a higher percentage of cocoa than classic milk chocolate. Milk smoothes some of the bitter notes in high-cocoa dark chocolate, making this variety the perfect starting point for the milk-chocolate lover looking to explore more nuanced flavours.

SIGNS OF QUALITY
- **Dark milk** chocolate should be deep brown in colour, featuring rich, cocoa-heavy notes of flavour.

FLAVOURED MILK

There are two ways to enhance and complement chocolate with flavourings. Some makers add powdered flavours (such as freeze-dried fruit or spices) directly into the conching process. For intense bursts of flavour, makers may choose to mix additions, such as pieces of fruit or sea salt flakes, into chocolate once it is tempered.

SIGNS OF QUALITY
- **Flavourings** should subtly complement the flavour of the cocoa beans, creating a well-rounded flavour profile.

UNUSUAL MILK

Some makers alter the flavour and texture of chocolate by replacing cow's milk with more unusual milks. Sheep's and goat's milks are popular, and buffalo's milk makes very creamy chocolate due to its high fat content. For vegans or those with a dairy intolerance, look out for almond, coconut, and rice-milk chocolate.

SIGNS OF QUALITY
- **Strong-flavoured milks**, such as goat's milk, should be balanced with a higher cocoa content.

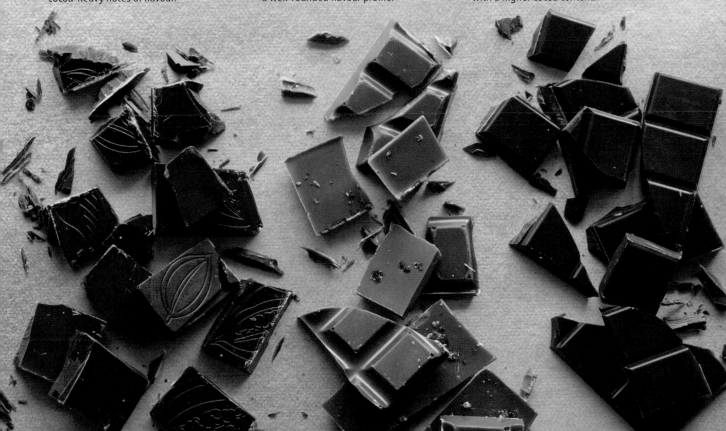

WHITE CHOCOLATE SPECTRUM

White chocolate was first made in the 1930s as a way to use up excess cocoa butter created during cocoa powder production. Today, chocolate makers continue to play with the flavour possibilities of white chocolate, and there are more varieties to choose from than ever.

20–30% milk powder

35% cocoa butter

35–45% sugar

COCOA CONTROVERSY

The debate as to whether white chocolate is actually chocolate has raged since it was first created. The key ingredients in white chocolate are cocoa butter, sugar, and milk powder – the controversy stems from the fact that it doesn't contain any cocoa solids. Around 54 per cent of the weight of a cocoa bean is cocoa butter, but the butter has little discernable flavour. Of course, whether white chocolate is chocolate or not doesn't need to matter a great deal, as long as you enjoy eating it.

BETTER WITH BUTTER

Cocoa butter is made by pressing melted cocoa mass, made from 100 per cent cocoa beans, through fine mesh material in a hydraulic press. Cocoa butter leaks through the mesh, leaving behind "cocoa cake": the solid part of the bean used for making cocoa powder.

Commercial cocoa butters are then processed to remove their natural cocoa flavour – this is known as "deodorizing" the cocoa butter. When used for making white chocolate, the cocoa butter is then combined with sugar, milk powder, and often other powdered flavourings. As the cocoa butter itself has almost no flavour, it can serve as a good backdrop for other flavours and textures. "Inclusions" and added flavourings are popular. Craft chocolate makers are experimenting with undeodorized cocoa butter to create bars that taste more of the beans they were made from.

CLASSIC WHITE

Classic white chocolate is a smooth combination of smooth cocoa butter with sugar and creamy milk powder. The core flavours are quite simple, so vanilla powder is often added to the mix.

SIGNS OF QUALITY

- **White chocolate** should be somewhere between pale ivory and light gold in colour.
- **Craft white** chocolate made with undeodorized cocoa butter has a subtle flavour that shouldn't be overwhelmed by the other ingredients.

30–40% sugar

30% milk powder

30–35% sugar

30% milk powder

40% cocoa butter

20–30% milk powder

30% cocoa butter

5–10% flavouring

30–35% cocoa butter

5–10% flavouring

30–35% sugar

CARAMELIZED WHITE

Makers have started producing "caramelized" or "blond" chocolate made by heating the chocolate until the sugars caramelize. Caramelized chocolate has a syrup-like sweetness and toasted flavour.

SIGNS OF QUALITY

- **Caramelized white chocolate** is a pale gold colour – almost resembling fudge – with a smooth texture on the palate and a clean "snap" when broken.

WHITE WITH INCLUSIONS

"Inclusions", or solid pieces of flavouring, are popular with makers seeking to add interest to naturally bland-tasting white chocolate. Makers add flavourings, such as dried fruit, nuts, edible flowers, or cocoa nibs, after tempering the chocolate.

SIGNS OF QUALITY

- **Inclusions** should complement the smooth texture and sweet taste of the chocolate.

FLAVOURED WHITE

White chocolate is a blank canvas for flavour and colouring. Makers add powdered flavourings or essential oils to the chocolate during grinding and conching, allowing the flavours to meld with the chocolate.

SIGNS OF QUALITY

- **Powdered flavourings** shouldn't affect the glossy texture of the chocolate.

- **Flavoured chocolate** can look striking if colourful flavourings such as matcha or freeze-dried berry powders are used.

WHAT IS ORGANIC CHOCOLATE?

More and more consumers want to know where chocolate comes from, what ingredients go into it, and its ethical and environmental cost. Organic cocoa production is currently small, but supply is gradually catching up with today's increasing demand.

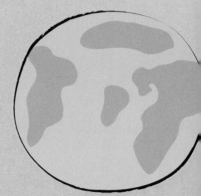

What do we mean by "organic"?

Precise definitions vary, but in general, the word "organic" refers to a crop that has been grown without chemicals or artificial fertilizers. In Europe, the US, and Australasia there are strict regulations surrounding the use of the term on a label – the product inside must contain at least 95 per cent organic ingredients and be certified by a recognized organization.

How much of the world's cocoa is organic?

According to the International Cocoa Organization (ICCO), organic cocoa represents just 0.5 per cent of production today. Most organic cocoa comes from countries associated with fine-flavoured chocolate, such as Madagascar, Bolivia, Brazil, and Costa Rica. Ivory Coast and Ghana, which produce the bulk of the world's cocoa, are notably absent from this list.

Why is it important?

The key benefit of organic chocolate is an environmental one. Most cocoa farmers live on or below the poverty line, in areas where there is little education. Because fertilizers and pesticides significantly increase yield, farmers are often motivated to use them. Without controls or training, chemicals are misused and may harm farmers, damage the environment, or find their way into chocolate.

Why is it so rare?

Going organic only makes sense for farmers if they can achieve a premium price for their crop. It's for this reason that organic cocoa is widely associated with craft chocolate makers, who prioritize quality and will pay more for organic cocoa. However, most organic certification programmes require a fee from cocoa farmers. Despite the benefits of carrying an official organic logo, many smaller producers find that this fee outweighs any advantages.

Does uncertified organic chocolate exist?

Some chocolate may be organic in all but name. This is particularly true in the craft chocolate world, where makers and farmers work together to produce the best possible chocolate.

RAW CHOCOLATE

Popular with the health-conscious for its alleged antioxidant-rich properties, raw chocolate is chocolate made with unroasted cocoa beans. By keeping temperatures low during production, makers can preserve naturally occuring antioxidants in the cocoa beans. Many products are now available, including bars, buttons, and powders.

THE RAW PROCESS

The subject of some controversy among chocolate experts, raw chocolate is made with unroasted cocoa beans. Makers often promote it as being higher in health-giving antioxidants and other minerals than traditionally processed chocolate.

Unfortunately, there is no legal definition of the term "raw", so it is difficult to know how a raw chocolate product has been made. Take time to research the maker before buying. With raw chocolate, it is vital that the beans are grown, selected, and processed hygienically, as they are not sterilized during the roasting stage.

HEALTHIER SNACKING?

Makers may claim that raw chocolate products are healthier than roasted ones. This is because they want to champion the health benefits of raw cocoa and the more general link between raw food and healthy eating. Look out for chocolate with sugar substitutes such as agave nectar or lucuma powder. There is also a wide variety of raw vegan products available, using coconut milk or nut powders to add creaminess.

A RAW DEAL?

Some experts argue that chocolate can never be truly raw. Heat is an essential part of its production process – from cacao growth and harvest, to fermentation and drying. Although beans remain unroasted, raw chocolate must also go through the same initial processes. Some makers also temper raw chocolate before selling it, and therefore melt it to 45°C (113°F). As such, raw chocolate might not meet all of your expectations of raw foods.

Raw milk chocolate is made with dairy milk powder just like roasted chocolate. Vegan milk substitutes are also popular.

Raw cocoa powder is made from unroasted cocoa beans that have been ground, then pressed to remove the cocoa butter. Raw cocoa powder is usually processed as little as possible to preserve antioxidants in the cocoa beans.

FLAVOUR AND TEXTURE

Like other chocolate, raw chocolate comes in many styles, flavours, and textures. Most raw chocolate has an earthy, grassy flavour due to the unroasted beans. Some raw chocolate makers try to keep processing to a minimum, so products may have a relatively coarse texture.

Raw chocolate with cocoa nibs shows off the raw base ingredient as well as smooth, processed chocolate. Cocoa nibs add extra texture and flavour to raw chocolate products.

Raw dark chocolate is often balanced with healthy sugar subsitutes to minimize acidity and boost citrus notes.

100% raw dark chocolate is not for the faint-hearted. Pure raw chocolate has an intense, slightly acidic flavour. Cocoa butter is often added to smooth out any harsh flavours.

Flavoured raw chocolate is often made with healthy inclusions to match its health credentials. Nutritious nuts, seeds, berries, and natural sweeteners are common additions.

THE CHOCOLATE SHOP

From its beginnings as a bitter drink made from hand-ground cocoa beans, chocolate is available in an array of shapes, sizes, and formats. More variety is available than ever, in specialist chocolate shops, supermarkets, and online.

THE MANY FACES OF CHOCOLATE

Chocolate has been around for thousands of years, but the chocolate bar as we know it wasn't invented until 1847. Since then, chocolate makers and chocolatiers around the world have made chocolate a ubiquitous part of daily life.

In the 21st century, it's craft chocolate makers who are changing the way we think about chocolate, creating exquisite bean-to-bar chocolate. Don't feel limited to what's on the supermarket shelves – visit a specialist chocolate shop, or go online to track down interesting varieties.

CRAFT CHOCOLATE BARS

Crafted from fine-flavour cocoa and quality ingredients, craft chocolate is produced to high ethical standards and promotes the true flavour and versatility of cocoa beans.

Look out for the phrase "bean to bar", the country of origin, and a short ingredients list on the label.

FRESH TRUFFLES AND FILLED CHOCOLATES

Hand-made bonbons are increasingly innovative; some use flavour pairings that complement the specific flavour notes in chocolate.

Look out for fresh truffles without preservatives. Choose good-quality truffles with a shelf life of 1–2 weeks.

SELECTION BOXES

Selection boxes can feature an impressive range of flavours and fillings.

Look out for simple, natural ingredients with minimal use of preservatives. The fillings may include vegetable fats, but make sure the chocolate itself contains cocoa butter.

CONFECTIONERY CHOCOLATE

Most chocolate available today is mass-produced confectionery, which often has a high sugar content.

Look out for a higher cocoa content (over 30 per cent for milk and 55 per cent for dark). Avoid chocolate with added vegetable fats, such as palm oil.

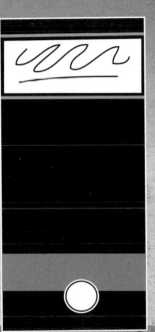

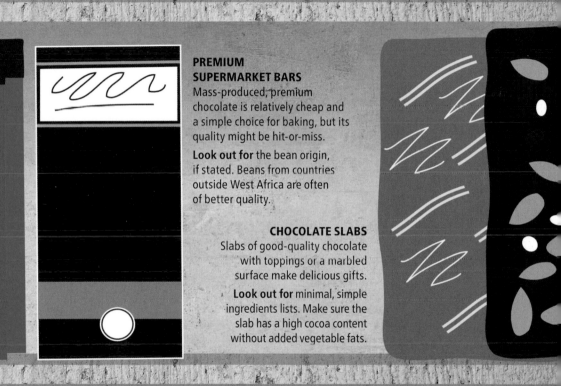

PREMIUM SUPERMARKET BARS

Mass-produced, premium chocolate is relatively cheap and a simple choice for baking, but its quality might be hit-or-miss.

Look out for the bean origin, if stated. Beans from countries outside West Africa are often of better quality.

CHOCOLATE SLABS

Slabs of good-quality chocolate with toppings or a marbled surface make delicious gifts.

Look out for minimal, simple ingredients lists. Make sure the slab has a high cocoa content without added vegetable fats.

HOT CHOCOLATE AND COCOA POWDER

Consumers can buy hot chocolate in many different formats and flavours. Cocoa powder comes in two different varieties – "natural" and "Dutch process".

Look out for proof that the hot chocolate is made from actual chocolate with minimal sugar and natural flavours. Choose the kind of cocoa powder that is specified in recipes – Dutch process cocoa powder has been treated to reduce acidity, giving a nutty flavour.

Behind the scenes | Laurent Gerbaud

THE CHOCOLATIER

Chocolatiers are perhaps the most revered figures in the chocolate world, and need years of training and experience to create perfect chocolates and confections. Belgian native Laurent Gerbaud honed his craft in Brussels and Shanghai before setting up his shop and café on Rue Ravenstein, in the heart of Brussels.

Employs six people: three in production, two in the shop, and one assistant

----

Studied at the Culinary School of Brussels (CERIA), Belgium

Laurent Gerbaud comes from several generations of bakers and pastry chefs, but it was only after making edible sculptures for a friend's art exhibition that Gerbaud realized he wanted to work with chocolate. He studied at the Culinary School of Brussels (CERIA) and apprenticed for two years with the French master chocolatier Frank Duval at Planète Chocolat, an experimental chocolaterie in Brussels.

After his apprenticeship, Gerbaud worked as a chocolatier in Shanghai, China. Inspired by the cuisines around him, he lost his taste for sugary chocolate, and focused instead on adding flavour and sweetness using dried fruit and roasted nuts. After two years, Gerbaud returned to Belgium, and in 2009 he opened his own shop in the centre of Brussels.

Today, Gerbaud sells filled chocolates, truffles, mendiants, and chocolate-dipped fruits with a focus on high-quality, traceable ingredients and meticulous flavour pairings. Gerbaud sources couverture from the Italian chocolate company Domori, using mainly dark chocolate made from Madagascan, Peruvian, and Ecuadorian cocoa beans. He is interested in making his own chocolate from cocoa beans in the future.

CHOCOLATE CHALLENGES

The demands of running a business as a chocolatier mean that most time must be spent on administrative tasks, rather than experimenting in the workshop. Gerbaud is allergic to a lot of the key ingredients in the chocolatier's storecupboard – uncooked nuts, as well as fresh apricots, figs, peaches, and kiwis – so he must take care when experimenting with recipes. This doesn't hinder his creativity, though – one of the shop's best-selling chocolates has a dried apricot filling.

A DAY IN THE LIFE

The shop and café is open for 9 hours a day, 7 days a week, so Gerbaud employs two assistants, as well as interacting with customers himself. He also supervises three assistant chocolatiers behind the scenes, who make chocolates using his recipes. One day a week, Gerbaud also works in production with his chocolatiers. He splits the rest of his time between running workshops, developing new products and packaging, sales, press and public relations, and accounting duties.

WORKSHOPS
Several times a week, Gerbaud runs making and tasting workshops at the shop for groups of 10–20 people.

MAKING MENDIANTS
Mendiants are a speciality at Gerbaud's shop. He makes them by tempering chocolate and topping them with dried fruit and nuts.

CHOCOLATE BOXES
Gerbaud's hand-made chocolates contain no added sugar, preservatives, artificial flavours, or additives.

DARK CHOCOLATE
Gerbaud's dark chocolate is made from Ecuadorian or Madagascan cocoa beans. His moulds feature the distinctive logo – a seal with the word "chocolate" in Mandarin.

IS CHOCOLATE GOOD FOR ME?

While many people consider chocolate to be a forbidden indulgence that does more harm than good, current research points to significant and diverse benefits of regular chocolate consumption. If your chocolate of choice is high-sugar and high-fat confectionery, try weaning yourself onto chocolate with a higher cocoa content instead to feel the benefits.

ARE THERE ANY BENEFITS OF EATING CHOCOLATE?

Yes! Many studies have found that consuming a small amount of good-quality dark chocolate with a high cocoa content every day can benefit your health. However, if you eat chocolate that is high in sugar, dairy, and other added ingredients, these will probably negate any benefits.

WHAT'S ALL THIS ABOUT ANTIOXIDANTS?

Chocolate is particularly high in antioxidant chemicals called flavanols. These help protect against free radicals, which are linked to cell damage. Regular intake of antioxidants has been shown to be particularly helpful for lowering blood pressure and preventing heart disease.

CAN IT FIGHT CANCER?

Chocolate certainly isn't a cure for cancer, but recent research has indicated that compounds present in chocolate could reduce the number of aberrant cells that are linked to colon cancer. Other studies have indicated chemicals present in chocolate may play a role in helping to prevent some forms of cancer.

WHY DO I LIKE IT SO MUCH?

Consuming chocolate can replicate the feeling of wellbeing we experience when falling in love. Theobromine, along with other chemicals found in chocolate, has been shown to release endorphins – pleasure-giving chemicals that are released during activities such as sex, exercise, and socialising.

IS CHOCOLATE BAD FOR MY TEETH?

Contrary to what you might think, chocolate could actually be good for your teeth. Recent research by Tulane University in Louisiana has shown that the theobromine found in chocolate is even better at strengthening teeth than fluoride. Unfortunately, the large quantities of sugar added to most chocolate can have quite the opposite effect.

IS IT A SUPERFOOD?

Sadly no, it's not a superfood or a miracle cure for any ailment. The sugar and fats present in the average confectionery bar are likely to have a negative impact on your health. Ditching prescribed medicines in favour of a bar of chocolate is certainly not a good idea, but enjoying some high-quality dark chocolate – in moderation – can be good for your body and mind.

CHOCOLATE CRAVINGS

There's no doubt that people love chocolate. Globally, we consume over seven million tonnes of it each year, and spend an estimated US$110 billion to feed our "need" for chocolate. But what is it that gives us chocolate cravings, and can chocolate really be addictive?

CHOCOHOLICS

The idea of a person being addicted to chocolate – a "chocoholic" – has been present in popular culture since the 1960s. The term tends to be used jokingly by self-declared chocolate lovers, rather than to imply a real addiction, but it is the apparently "addictive" appeal of chocolate that has attracted so much scientific attention to the food.

THE CHEMISTRY OF CHOCOLATE

Cocoa beans contain several chemicals that are associated with enhancing our mood and sense of wellbeing. Tryptophan, anandamide, and phenylethylamine are known to have a positive impact on mood – but they're present in chocolate in such small quantities that they may be broken down before reaching the brain.

Theobromine, a chemical found in chocolate in relatively large quantities, has a similar chemical structure to caffeine and has been found to increase the heart rate and relax blood vessels. Very small amounts of theobromine can be found in yerba mate, guarana berries, and kola nuts, but is most prevalent in cocoa beans, hence its name: "theobromine", after *Theobroma*, the cacao tree. Studies suggest that the physical effects of theobromine, while not as pronounced as those of caffeine, may have mildly addictive qualities.

PSYCHOLOGICAL VS PHYSIOLOGICAL

Although chocolate does contain chemicals proven to have an effect on the brain, the quantities in a single bar are so small that the chances of becoming physiologically addicted to chocolate are slim.

There is, however, more to how we experience chocolate than chemical reactions. Chocolate melts just below body temperature, meaning it turns to liquid and releases its intense, sweet flavour almost as soon as it hits the tongue. This pleasurable sensory experience may well contribute to chocolate's appeal.

We often associate chocolate with temptation and indulgence, and this may make "giving in" to it all the more fun – it is the attraction of the forbidden apple. This psychological element may play a bigger part in "chocoholism" than is commonly acknowledged.

CONTROL THE CRAVINGS

If you find yourself craving chocolate, try to opt for quality. Good-quality dark chocolate has scientifically proven health benefits. It includes less sugar and a higher cocoa content than mass-produced milk chocolate, meaning you'll also need less chocolate to feel satisfied.

DARK CHOCOLATE
Dark varieties feature high quantities of theobromine, which may contribute to any "addictive" qualities.

TASTE

Bursting with complex flavours and aromas, chocolate rewards those who take time to appreciate it. Learn how to make the most of each bite with the help of professional tasting techniques.

HOW TO TASTE CHOCOLATE

Tasting chocolate involves so much more than just eating it. By slowing down the experience and using all your senses (as shown on pp126–27), you will uncover flavours, aromas, textures, and hidden complexities, and learn to truly appreciate the skill of the chocolate maker.

ENHANCE THE TASTE

Chocolate is one of the most complex and exciting foods in the world, with more than 400 identifiable flavour notes. The melting point of chocolate is only a couple of degrees below the temperature of the human body, meaning that its flavours start to appear the moment that it hits your tongue. Learning to taste chocolate effectively is about maximizing the time these flavours, aromas, and textures have to develop.

TASTING IN THE INDUSTRY

Tasting chocolate is a serious business and an essential skill for those working in the chocolate industry. Professional tasters hone their skills over years and are able to pick out individual flavour notes, aromas, and characteristics of texture. Tasters can identify potential flaws, helping chocolate makers and chocolatiers improve their products. Chocolate makers, chocolatiers, chefs, and professional tasters must rely on their tasting skills to develop products and spot any flaws in existing ones.

KEEP IT FUN

Chocolate can taste sensational even when you don't take the time to analyze it, so as a chocolate enthusiast, you might be wondering: why does it matter? By learning how to get the most from chocolate, you can significantly enhance the

Why so intense?

Is it creamy?

THE FLAVOUR PROCESS

Every stage of the chocolate-making process affects the flavour of chocolate. From the cacao variety, soil conditions, and climate, through to fermentation and drying, many characteristics are locked in before the beans even reach the chocolate maker. The maker's skill lies in bringing out the best in the cocoa bean and encouraging fine flavour by carefully controlling the roasting, grinding, and conching processes.

whole experience. If you understand the origins of chocolate and how it is made, you can also make more informed buying decisions. Learning to taste chocolate properly is an exciting way to understand flavour and improve your palate, but make sure you keep it fun. While it is easy to get drawn into the world of fine flavour and aroma, chocolate does, after all, exist for pleasure.

Taste it slow

Foods can taste very different when you eat them at different speeds, and chocolate is no exception. Taste a piece of chocolate quickly, then slowly, and you may discover a new experience.

1 Take two pieces of the same dark chocolate and eat the first one quickly. Chew it a couple of times and swallow.

2 Cleanse your palate with water and taste the second one slowly, taking in the aroma and letting it melt.

3 Note your results. Often you will find that chocolate tastes sweeter when you eat it a little more slowly. By taking your time and taking in the full aroma, you're giving the natural flavour notes time to develop. Most chocolates taste significantly better when consumed more slowly and allowed to melt in the mouth.

Does it MELT?

TASTING WITH YOUR SENSES

According to scientific research, the majority of the flavour we experience when tasting foods comes from aroma rather than what we taste on the tongue. When it comes to enjoying chocolate, taste and aroma are just the start of the story – to fully appreciate it you also need to examine its appearance, texture, and finish.

THE TASTING JOURNEY

Great chocolate will take you on a journey. Unwrapping and tasting it for the first time is a sensory experience that uncovers the skill of the maker and reveals the quality of the ingredients. To fully appreciate it, you need to take your time and use all of your senses.

Start your chocolate tasting with a clean palate and cleanse it between each piece of chocolate. You can simply drink a little water, but savoury biscuits and pieces of apple are also great palate-cleansers.

1 See

Unwrap your bar of chocolate for the first time. You should see a beautiful, glossy sheen. This is a sign that the chocolate has been well tempered and that it has been stored in optimal conditions. If the chocolate is dull or has a white bloom, it could be a sign of poor tempering or that the chocolate has been stored somewhere too warm or too cold.

1. SEE...

2 Hear

Break your chocolate into pieces. The sound it makes when you do this is a sign of quality – it should break with a clean "snap" sound. Tempering helps form the perfect crystal structure. Well-tempered chocolate makes an audible snap and is likely to melt in the mouth at the perfect rate to release a full range of flavour.

2. HEAR...

snap!

3 Smell

Cup a piece of chocolate in your hand and bring it close to your nose before inhaling. When you first unwrap a bar, you'll almost certainly experience some of what the chocolate has to offer as the aroma is released for the first time, but to experience the full aroma, you should get closer to the chocolate. Aroma is vital for experiencing the full flavour of chocolate, so it's important to make the most of it.

4 Touch

Place the chocolate on your tongue and allow it to melt. Good chocolate should have a smooth, silky texture when placed on the tongue. A smooth and well-tempered chocolate will melt evenly over the tongue without leaving residue behind.

A BURST OF FLAVOUR

Are you having trouble identifying a flavour or aroma? Here's a simple trick to maximize both. Allow a piece of chocolate to melt on your tongue for a few moments, holding your nose. Once it has melted, release your nose, inhale, and you should experience a more intense burst of aroma and flavour.

5 Taste

Identify some of the distinct flavour notes as they develop. If the chocolate releases flavour too slowly, bite it a couple of times, but try not to chew. Is it nutty, fruity, or floral? What kind of fruit does it remind you of? It's not always easy to put flavours into words – a flavour wheel is a good tool for identifying subtle nuances (see pp128–29).

TASTING WHEELS

Chocolate offers an incredible range of complex aromas and tastes. Identify the subtleties of flavour with the help of these wheels, and get the best from your tasting experience. You can improve your palate with a little practice – the more you try, the easier it is to differentiate between varieties of chocolate.

IDENTIFYING CHARACTERISTICS

Use these at-a-glance wheels as prompts to help you to put chocolate's flavours, aromas, and textures into words. Follow the directions for tasting chocolate on pp126–27, and keep a note of common characteristics as you taste.

With a food as complex as chocolate, these two wheels can't cover the entire spectrum of factors that you might experience. For instance, chocolate may be astringent or bitter, or have a high level of acidity. Keep a note of this too, and whether you find it appealing or not. Consider the "finish" – the lingering flavour that stays with you after the chocolate has gone.

TEXTURE WHEEL

Chocolate texture is an important factor in tasting. Most manufacturers try to make sure that their chocolate has a very smooth texture, for the best possible melt. Adding cocoa butter produces a smoother chocolate that melts more quickly. However, some makers go for a different approach, coarsely grinding their cocoa and sugar for an unrefined, biscuit-like texture. Use the wheel below to consider the texture of each chocolate and how it affects the overall experience.

THERE ARE MORE THAN 400 DISTINCT FLAVOUR NOTES IN CHOCOLATE

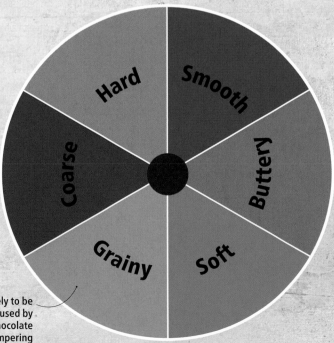

A grainy texture is likely to be a defect, sometimes caused by moisture mixing with chocolate during conching or tempering

FLAVOUR WHEEL

Identify key flavours in the chocolate using the flavour wheel, honing in on more specific profiles. Make a note of the prominent flavour notes and how quickly the chocolate melts on the tongue.

Earthy flavours are quite common in many types of Ecuadorian chocolate

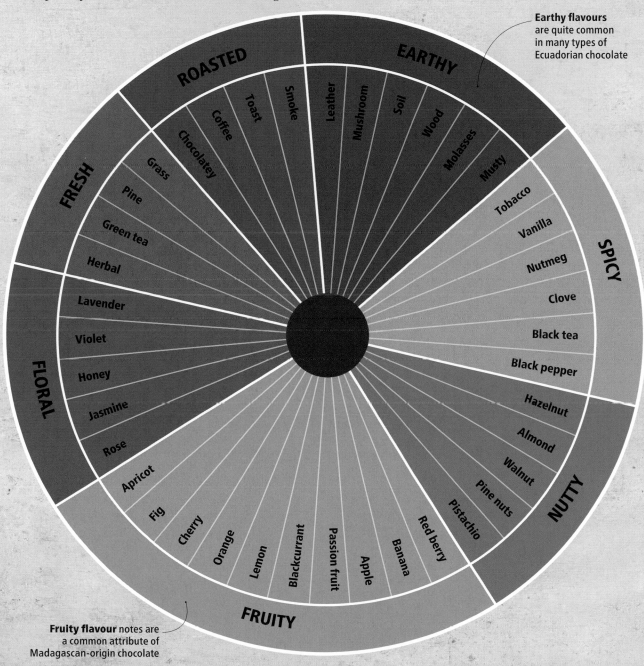

Fruity flavour notes are a common attribute of Madagascan-origin chocolate

PAIRING WITH FLAVOURS

Chocolate's diverse natural flavours lend themselves to pairing with many types of food and drink. Wines, fruit, cheeses, and beers can all make delicious pairings for chocolate. Identify the flavour profiles of your favourite bars (see pp128–29), then select pairings that complement or contrast with those flavours.

COMPLEMENTARY

roasted peanuts whisky
roasted almonds coffee cocoa nibs

CHOCOLATE FLAVOUR **ROASTED**

marzipan red wine (Pinot Noir or Merlot)
porter
stout

CONTRASTING

COMPLEMENTARY

mild goat's cheese
green tea soft cheese
fresh pears

CHOCOLATE FLAVOUR **FRESH**

fresh red berries
dried figs
rosé

CONTRASTING

COMPLEMENTARY

berry tea
white wine (Gewurztraminer, Riesling, or Chenin Blanc)
floral tea

CHOCOLATE FLAVOUR **FLORAL**

pale ale soft cheese
sparkling wine cider
lager rosé

CONTRASTING

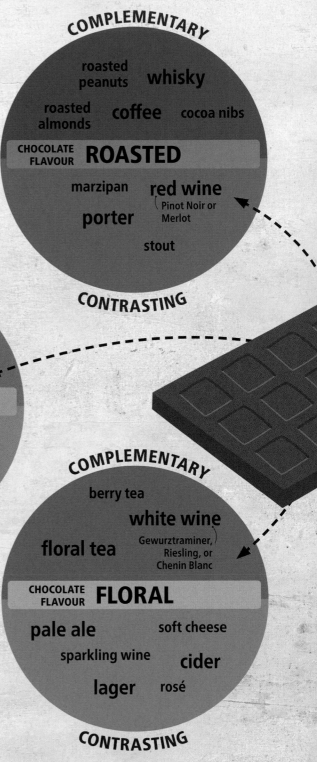

ORGANIZE A TASTING PARTY
Pairing events are a fun way to experiment with matching flavour to different types of chocolate. Pick between three and five good-quality chocolate bars, and pair each of them with a different food or drink, using this page for inspiration. Discuss how well the pairings work, and brainstorm new pairing ideas.

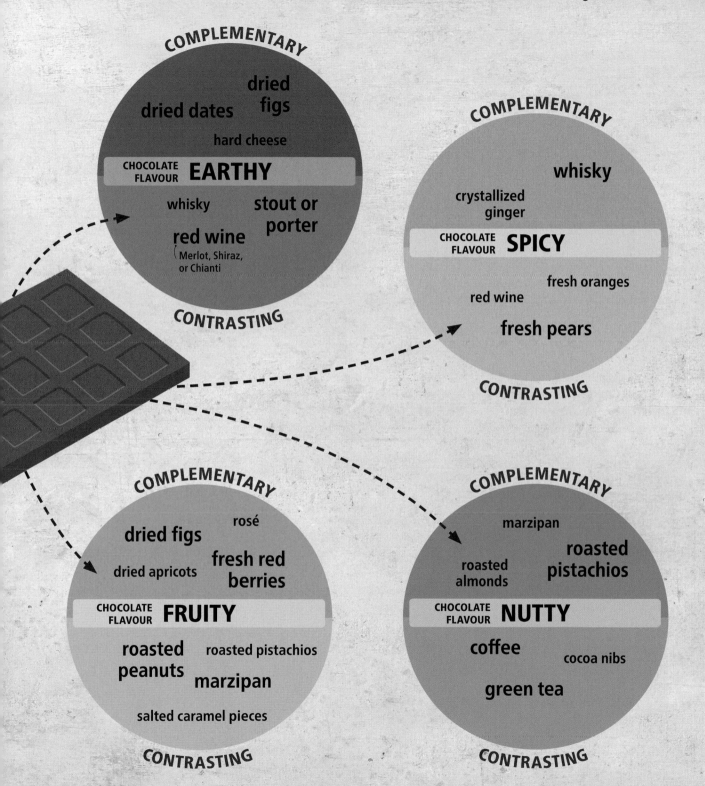

COMPLEMENTARY

dried dates · dried figs

hard cheese

CHOCOLATE FLAVOUR **EARTHY**

whisky · stout or porter

red wine
(Merlot, Shiraz, or Chianti)

CONTRASTING

COMPLEMENTARY

whisky

crystallized ginger

CHOCOLATE FLAVOUR **SPICY**

fresh oranges

red wine

fresh pears

CONTRASTING

COMPLEMENTARY

dried figs · rosé

dried apricots · fresh red berries

CHOCOLATE FLAVOUR **FRUITY**

roasted peanuts · roasted pistachios

marzipan

salted caramel pieces

CONTRASTING

COMPLEMENTARY

marzipan

roasted almonds · roasted pistachios

CHOCOLATE FLAVOUR **NUTTY**

coffee · cocoa nibs

green tea

CONTRASTING

Behind the scenes | Jennifer Earle

THE PROFESSIONAL TASTER

Chocolate tasters assess the array of chocolate products on the market, bringing the best products to the public. Jennifer Earle has been tasting chocolate professionally since 2006, and runs Chocolate Ecstasy Tours, which introduce enthusiasts to fine chocolate in London and Brighton.

Since 2005, Earle has run chocolate tours in London and Brighton

----

Judge of many industry awards, including the International Chocolate Awards and Great Taste Awards

Jennifer Earle grew up Australia and travelled the world in her early twenties. It was during her travels that she was inspired to set up a chocolate tour company in the UK. Called Chocolate Ecstasy Tours, the company introduces locals and visitors to the variety of high-quality chocolate available in London. By introducing people to the joys of high-quality chocolate bars and confections, Earle hopes to educate the public in the importance of sustainably grown and ethically produced chocolate. The business has grown gradually, and Earle's chocolate-tasting expertise has attracted the attention of large food companies, who have employed her as a food buyer and product developer.

Today, Earle runs her business full-time in both Brighton and London, as well as working as a professional chocolate taster for chocolate companies and chocolate competitions, including the International Chocolate Awards, the Academy of Chocolate Awards, and the Great Taste Awards. Earle has had professional sensory training to help hone her taste buds for the role.

CHOCOLATE CHALLENGES

Most chocolate-tasting is unpaid, so it can be difficult to find enough qualified tasters to assess the quantity of entrants, and professional tasters such as Earle must also work elsewhere in order to make a living. Chocolate-tasting introduces Earle to some of the best chocolate in the world, but judging competitions can be exhausting – each mouthful must be carefully savoured and analyzed, to ensure that every product is assessed fairly.

A DAY IN THE LIFE

Chocolate competitions are judged by a panel of tasters – a good panel will have people from a variety of tasting backgrounds, including some with less professional experience who represent the perspective of a typical consumer. On an average day of tasting, Earle judges different categories of chocolate bars, filled chocolates, and truffles as part of a panel of experts. She makes notes on each variety, and awards marks for characteristics. At the end of the competition, the marks from the panel are totted up to reveal the winners.

CHOCOLATE TASTING
In each category, Earle awards marks for taste, appearance, aroma, and texture.

THE LONDON CHOCOLATE SHOW
Earle is regularly asked to speak about her role as a chocolate taster at industry events, such as The London Chocolate Show, which takes place once a year.

PRODUCT SELECTION
In a tasting, there are usually 4–5 varieties of chocolate products per category, but sometimes there can be as many as 15 varieties.

INTERNATIONAL CHOCOLATE AWARDS
Tasters drink water and eat tiny quantities of cold, cooked polenta to cleanse their palates between each product. There is a 40-minute break between each round to allow the panel's aroma and taste sensitivities to recover.

HOW SHOULD I STORE CHOCOLATE?

Look beyond the "best before" date to discover how to keep your chocolate at its best for longer. Properly stored, a good-quality bar of chocolate can last a year or more; filled chocolates or truffles made with fresh cream may only last a week.

SHOULD I KEEP CHOCOLATE COOL?

Chocolate melts at around 34°C (93°F). It only takes a few moments in direct sunlight for the cocoa butter in the chocolate to melt and cause bloom. You should store chocolate at a constant temperature – aim for a cool room temperature, between 15 and 20°C (59 and 68°F).

SHOULD I KEEP IT IN THE FRIDGE?

No! One of the biggest mistakes people make with chocolate is storing it in the fridge. Condensation can quickly form on the surface of the chocolate, softening its texture and drawing the sugars to the surface to form sugar bloom.

WHAT ABOUT A FOOD CUPBOARD?

Yes, this is fine, as long as the chocolate is in a sealed airtight plastic container. Ensure that it is kept dry and away from moisture. Chocolate tends to take on the aromas of anything it's stored with, so always keep your chocolate away from strong smells – this includes other, strongly flavoured chocolates.

HOW SHOULD I KEEP CHOCOLATE LIKE AN EXPERT?

If you're serious about chocolate and want to build up a collection of bars, consider investing in a wine fridge. A modern wine fridge can be adjusted to around 18°C (64°F) – the ideal temperature for storing chocolate. Replace the wire racks with shelves and you have the perfect storage solution for chocolate.

HOW SHOULD I KEEP FILLED CHOCOLATES AND TRUFFLES?

Always check the label. Most artisan chocolatiers use fresh cream and no preservatives, resulting in a very short shelf life. Expect fresh chocolates to have a shelf life of 1–2 weeks at most. Proper storage will help to maximize that time, but always pay attention to the "use by" date.

I'M BUYING BEANS. HOW SHOULD I KEEP THEM?

Although not as sensitive to temperature variations as chocolate, beans should be kept in a cool, dry place away from odours. Unroasted cocoa beans can carry bacteria, so it's important to keep them away from roasted beans, cocoa nibs, and chocolate. Once roasted, beans and nibs should be stored in airtight containers.

CREATE

Become a bean-to-bar chocolate maker and master your own truffles, bark, and chocolates. Step-by-step techniques guide you through every stage in the process, helping you to achieve sweet success.

FROM BEAN TO BAR

With simple tools you can create your own bars of chocolate from raw cocoa beans. On the following pages is a step-by-step guide to making dark chocolate, but it is easy to adapt this method for making milk and white chocolate, too.

Hairdryer

Grinder

Milk powder

Unrefined cane sugar

Cocoa butter

Cocoa beans

Chocolate moulds

Digital food thermometer

Marble slab

Grinder
This grinds and conches roasted cocoa beans into liquid chocolate over a period of days. Table-top wet grinders – used in India to prepare *dosa* – are perfect for making small batches of chocolate at home. They are now available to buy relatively cheaply online.

Hairdryer
Essential for winnowing and tempering, this is one of the most useful pieces of equipment that the home chocolate maker can own. Choose one with a cold air setting.

Milk powder
This is only necessary if you are making milk or white chocolate. Choose a milk powder that is free from additives – not baby formula.

Unrefined cane sugar
You can use refined sugar in chocolate-making, but unrefined sugar tastes much better. Grind it with the cocoa nibs over a long period of time to create liquid chocolate.

Cocoa butter
This smoothes chocolate, making it easy to work with. It's available in pellets or slabs – melt it before adding to the grinder.

Cocoa beans
The core ingredient in dark and milk chocolate. Buy the best beans you can afford; bags weighing 1–2kg (2¼–4½ lb) are available from specialist wholesalers. Single-origin beans from Central and South America, the Caribbean, and Madagascar have the best flavour.

Chocolate moulds
You can use thin, flexible plastic moulds or recycled food containers to shape tempered chocolate, but if you're serious about chocolate-making, invest in polycarbonate moulds from specialist websites.

Digital food thermometer
This is vital for accurate temperature control when tempering chocolate. Use an accurate digital thermometer with a prong – this will give you more reliable readings.

Marble slab
Traditionally used by chocolatiers, a marble or granite slab is an optional piece of equipment used to cool chocolate during tempering.

ROASTING

For the chocolate maker, the first stage in the bean-to-bar process is roasting. Roasting brings out the natural flavours in the cocoa beans and doesn't require any specialized equipment. The temperature and duration of a roast changes depending on the beans, your oven, and your personal taste (see box, below). Just take care not to burn the beans.

WHAT YOU NEED

TIME
10–30 mins

SPECIAL EQUIPMENT
hairdryer with cold setting
  or desktop fan

INGREDIENTS
1kg (2¼ lb) cocoa beans

2 Cover a large baking tray with the cocoa beans in a single layer – this ensures an even roast. Place the tray in the preheated oven and start a timer (see box, below).

1 Preheat the oven (see box, right). Spread the beans out on a board or tray, and pick out and discard any debris, such as twigs or small stones. Remove any beans with holes, or any that are broken, flat, or have a significantly different colour.

TIME AND TEMPERATURE

Start by roasting your beans for 20 minutes at 140°C (275°F). Then taste the beans and adjust the roast accordingly – 10–30 minutes and 120°C–160°C (250°F–325°F) is a good window for experimentation. Take notes on each roast, so that you have a reference point for any adjustments you would like to make.

ROASTING COCOA BEANS DEVELOPS FLAVOURS, STERILIZES THEM, AND LOOSENS THE PAPERY SHELLS

The shell is thin and papery and should peel away easily from the nib

The nib is usually darker in colour than the shell, with a crumbly texture

3 Once you've roasted the beans, remove them from the oven and transfer them to another cool tray. Use a hairdryer or desktop fan to blow cold air over the beans for a few minutes until the beans have cooled. As long as the beans are hot, they will continue to roast, so it's important to cool them as quickly as possible.

4 Take a bean and break it open with your fingers. Discard the shell and taste a piece of the nib, observing the flavours. Too smoky and you have probably roasted for too long, so reduce the time a little on your next batch. If the bean tastes overly acidic or grassy, try increasing the roast time by a minute or two.

BREAKING AND WINNOWING

Once you've roasted your beans, the next step in the process is to break and "winnow" them. Winnowing is the process of removing the papery outer shells to leave behind the cocoa nibs. For the home chocolate maker, the quickest way to achieve this is to crush the beans and then use a hairdryer to blow away the lighter shells, leaving the heavier nibs behind.

WHAT YOU NEED

TIME
35–40 mins

SPECIAL EQUIPMENT
large plastic food bag

hairdryer with cold setting

INGREDIENTS
approx. 1kg (2¼lb) cocoa beans,
 sorted, roasted, and cooled
 (see pp140–141)

1 Transfer the cocoa beans, a few handfuls at a time, into a large plastic food bag. Hit them with a rolling pin, taking care not to pierce the bag, until every bean is crushed. Alternatively, place the beans in a large bowl and crush them with the end of a rolling pin.

2 Tip the broken beans into a large bowl. Turn the hairdryer on to a cool, low setting. Slowly bring the hairdryer towards the bowl so that the shells start to blow away from the surface of the beans. This part of the process makes a lot of mess, so you might choose to do it outside.

THE COCOA NIBS

A cocoa nib is simply a piece of broken, shelled cocoa bean. You can make nibs by roasting, breaking, and winnowing cocoa beans yourself, or you can buy them ready-processed, in roasted form. You could use them as a satisfyingly crunchy, antioxidant-rich addition to savoury and sweet recipes.

WINNOWING TRANSFORMS COCOA BEANS INTO COCOA NIBS

THE SHELLS

Some chocolate makers infuse a "cocoa tea" from the waste cocoa shells; others use them as garden mulch. When making chocolate at home, it is best to dispose of the shells safely, as they may contain contaminants left over from the fermentation and drying process. Chocolate is poisonous to some animals, particularly dogs. If you keep animals, it is best not to dispose of the shells in the garden.

3 Gently shake the bowl or stir the beans to bring more shells to the surface. Move the hairdryer around to find the best angle to blow away the shells without losing any nibs. If you spot any remaining unbroken beans, remove them and crush them using the rolling pin.

4 Keep stirring or shaking the bowl to bring more shells to the surface, blowing the beans constantly with the hairdryer. After 15–20 minutes, you will be left with a bowl full of cocoa nibs and very little shell. Remove any remaining pieces of shell by hand.

GRINDING AND CONCHING

To turn cocoa nibs into dark chocolate, you need to grind them with sugar. The friction created by the grinder melts and releases the cocoa butter in the nibs, transforming them into liquid chocolate. The continual stirring motion "conches" the chocolate, eradicating moisture and bad-tasting volatile elements.

WHAT YOU NEED

TIME
at least 24 hrs

SPECIAL EQUIPMENT
table-top wet grinder (see p138)
hairdryer

INGREDIENTS
800g (1¾lb) roasted cocoa nibs (see pp140–43)

400g (14oz) unrefined cane sugar

125g (4½oz) cocoa butter

15g (½oz) powdered flavourings (optional; see p148)

Gradually add the cocoa nibs into the grinder

1 Turn the grinder on and slowly start adding the cocoa nibs into the grinder, a little at a time, until all the nibs have been added. Keep the grinder running constantly throughout the process.

RECIPES FOR SUCCESS

Here are some suggested recipes to get you started. Weigh all your ingredients, including the cocoa nibs, before you start. Calculate the percentages of sugar and milk powder carefully, taking notes so that you can refine the recipe for future batches.

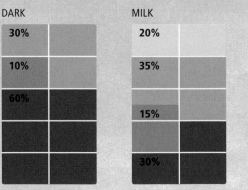

DARK	MILK	WHITE
30%	20%	30%
10%	35%	
60%	15%	35%
		35%
	30%	

KEY
- ■ Cocoa nibs
- ■ Cocoa butter
- □ Milk powder
- ■ Unrefined cane sugar

2 Use a spatula to dislodge build-up around the wheels of the grinder. Heat the inside and outside of the grinder drum for a few minutes using the hairdryer on a warm setting. This will speed up the melting of the beans and help to prevent blockages.

The science bit

Grinding the chocolate gradually reduces the particle size of the nibs and sugar to less than 30 microns – 0.03mm ($\frac{1}{800}$ in) – in diameter. This gives the chocolate a smooth texture, with particles so small that you cannot discern them on the palate. Conching forms a chemical reaction that reduces volatile elements, minimizing acidity and giving chocolate a rounded, developed flavour.

Add the sugar slowly, so that the grinder doesn't jam

A small amount of cocoa butter will make the chocolate smoother and easier to work with

4 Heat the cocoa butter in an ovenproof jug in the oven at 50ºC (120ºF) for about 15 minutes, until it has just melted. Take care not to overheat the cocoa butter, as it could burn the chocolate. Gradually add the melted cocoa butter to the grinder.

3 After 1–2 hours of grinding, the cocoa nibs will have transformed into a liquid. Slowly add the sugar, a little at a time. Don't go too quickly, as the grinder may jam if the mixture becomes too thick too quickly.

5 If you are making a flavoured or milk chocolate, add milk powder and/or powdered flavourings to your chocolate (see p148), and continue the conching process. With powdered flavourings, start by adding a very small quantity and gradually add more to taste.

THE EXTRAS
Some chocolate makers add vanilla to their chocolate, to help improve the flavour, or lecithin, as an emulsifier. Neither of these ingredients is necessary when making chocolate at home. However, if you would like to add them, do not use liquid forms, such as vanilla extract. Adding liquid to your chocolate can cause it to seize and become unusable.

Test the chocolate for texture as well as flavour

6 For the best results, leave the grinder running for at least 24 hours. Taste the chocolate as you go along, to keep track of the development of flavours and texture, and to judge whether you'd like to add a little more of any of the additional ingredients.

GRINDING COCOA BEANS RELEASES COCOA BUTTER, REFINES NIBS AND SUGAR INTO TINY PARTICLES, AND CONCHES THE CHOCOLATE

7 When the chocolate is ready, turn the grinder off and remove the chocolate from the drum. Some grinders have a tilting mechanism that makes this easy. With other machines, you may have to lift the drum off the base in order to pour the chocolate out.

8 Pour the chocolate into a large plastic container, using a silicone spatula to scrape as much chocolate out of the drum as possible. Put the lid on and allow the chocolate to cool and set. Do not put the chocolate in the fridge, as condensation may form on the chocolate. You may wish to age your chocolate before tempering it (see p149).

WHAT'S YOUR FLAVOUR?

Once you've added sugar, cocoa butter, and – if you're making milk chocolate – milk powder to the cocoa nibs, you can sit back and let the grinder do the work. Alternatively, experiment by adding flavours to the mix (see step 5, p146).

For the best results, find ingredients that pair well with the natural flavour notes in your cocoa. Some beans are naturally citrussy and acidic, while others may have earthy or floral notes. Any additional flavourings, should work with the chocolate, not against it. Always add powdered flavourings to your chocolate, never liquids – it only takes a few drops of liquid to cause a batch of chocolate to seize completely.

Powdered flavourings, such as spices and freeze-dried fruit powders, should be added to the grinder during step 5 of Grinding and conching (see p146). The particles will refine down with the cocoa nibs and sugar, ensuring that your chocolate is wonderfully smooth. Add your flavourings, a little at a time and taste regularly. You can always add more, but you can't take them out! Chunkier flavourings, such as nuts and dried fruit, can be added after the chocolate has been ground, conched, and tempered (see pp156–7).

Sea salt heightens many flavours in chocolate

Freeze-dried raspberry powder complements fruity notes in chocolate

Chilli powder adds a heat kick to high cocoa-content chocolate

Liquorice powder pairs well with creamy chocolate

Freeze-dried passion fruit powder is zingy and refreshing, cutting through the richness of chocolate

THE WAITING GAME

Flavour development doesn't stop when the grinding and conching is over. If you're serious about chocolate-making, you might want to age the chocolate for a few weeks before working with it. When you make chocolate from bean to bar, without artificial additives or preservatives, the flavours will continue to develop for weeks after you've poured it out of the grinder. Once your chocolate block has set completely in the container, tip it out, wrap it in cling film, and put it away in a cool, dry place for 2–3 weeks. This stage of the process isn't essential, but it will give your chocolate a more consistent and developed flavour. Most craft chocolate makers store their chocolate for several weeks in block form before tempering it and using it for bars.

AGEING FOR A FEW WEEKS IMPARTS A CONSISTENT FINAL FLAVOUR

Chocolate tends to absorb the flavours and aromas around it, so store it away from strong flavours and smells. You can also exploit this property to add even more flavour by storing your chocolate in airtight containers with other ingredients. Craft chocolate makers are ageing blocks of their chocolate with pieces of wood from whisky barrels, for example – this process imparts a subtle flavour to the finished chocolate.

TEMPERING

Master the art of tempering to transform chocolate into shiny, professional-looking, and long-lasting bars and confections. The chocolate must be carefully heated, cooled, and heated again to alter the crystalline structure (see box, opposite). Melt chocolate over a bain-marie, and either heat it with a hairdryer (see below) or spread it out on a heat-absorbent surface (see pp152–53).

MODERN TEMPERING

The simplest tempering method for the home chocolate maker is to heat the chocolate over a pan of simmering water (bain-marie), cool it, then gently and slowly heat it again with a hairdryer. Don't worry if it doesn't work perfectly – you can re-temper as many times as you need. Take care not to allow steam or water to come into contact with the chocolate, or it will seize and become unworkable.

WHAT YOU NEED

TIME
1 hr

SPECIAL EQUIPMENT
digital food thermometer
hairdryer

INGREDIENTS
500g (1lb 2oz) dark
   chocolate, roughly
   chopped

1 Melt the chocolate using a bain-marie: place it in a heatproof bowl over a small saucepan of gently simmering water. Make sure the bottom of the bowl doesn't touch the surface of the water. As it melts, stir the chocolate with a silicone spatula every two minutes or so.

2 Once the chocolate has melted, keep the thermometer in the chocolate at all times and check it regularly – accurate temperature control is key to a good temper. Stir the chocolate regularly with the spatula until it reaches 45°C (113°F).

3 When the chocolate reaches 45°C (113°F) – or the right temperature for the kind of chocolate you are tempering (see box above) – immediately place the bowl of chocolate on top of a saucepan of cold water, and stir so that the temperature cools.

The science bit

Chemically speaking, chocolate is a suspension of cocoa and sugar particles in cocoa butter crystals. There are six different types of cocoa butter crystals present in chocolate: types I, II, III, IV, V, and VI. Each has different properties, but only type V gives the sheen and "snap" that makes beautiful chocolate. To temper chocolate, first heat it to the melting point of all crystal types. Then, cool it to the point where type IV and type V crystals form. Finally, heat it again to melt the type IV crystals, leaving just type V behind. Type VI does not form during the tempering process.

THE TEMPERATURE STAGES

Temper temperatures can vary slightly depending on the beans and other ingredients. Here are some basic guides for dark, milk, and white chocolate.

KEY
■ Dark
■ Milk
□ White

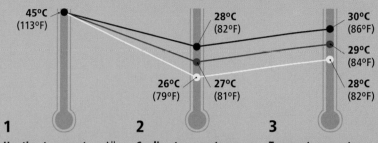

1
Heating temperature All chocolates should be melted initially to 45°C (113°F).

45°C (113°F)

2
Cooling temperature At this point, type IV and type V crystals will form.

28°C (82°F) · 26°C (79°F) · 27°C (81°F)

3
Temper temperature The type IV crystals will melt away, leaving type V.

30°C (86°F) · 29°C (84°F) · 28°C (82°F)

4 Monitor the temperature closely; when it falls to 28°C (82°F), remove the bowl from the saucepan. Gently reheat the chocolate with the hairdryer on a low heat setting. Stir the chocolate constantly with a silicone spatula, taking care not to overheat it.

5 Once the temperature reaches 30°C (86°F), it should be tempered and ready to use. Keep the chocolate at a constant temperature, stirring frequently, while you test the temper. Dip a small piece of baking parchment in the chocolate, and briefly transfer it to the fridge to set.

6 After three minutes, the chocolate on the parchment should be set and glossy. If there are streaks or greyness, start the process again from step 1. Use successfully tempered chocolate immediately.

TRADITIONAL TEMPERING

This traditional chocolatier's technique involves heating chocolate over a bain-marie and then cooling it slowly by spreading it on heat-absorbing marble. It is a tricky technique to master, but you can always re-temper if something goes wrong. With practice you will identify the right texture of perfectly tempered chocolate.

WHAT YOU NEED

TIME
30 mins

SPECIAL EQUIPMENT
marble or granite slab or surface, clean and dry

digital food thermometer

metal spatula or dough scraper (optional)

INGREDIENTS
500g (1lb 2oz) dark chocolate, roughly chopped

1 Melt the chocolate using a bain-marie: place it in a heatproof bowl over a small saucepan of gently simmering water. Make sure the bottom of the bowl doesn't touch the surface of the water. As it melts, stir the chocolate with a silicone spatula every two minutes or so.

2 Once the chocolate has melted, keep the thermometer in the chocolate at all times and check it regularly – accurate temperature control is key to a good temper. Stir the chocolate regularly with the spatula until it reaches 45ºC (113ºF).

MICROWAVE TEMPERING

If you're working with ready-made chocolate, such as chocolate bars or couverture chocolate, you can temper it in a microwave. Heat the chocolate in a microwaveable bowl, stopping every 20 seconds to stir the chocolate thoroughly. As the chocolate melts, reduce the amount of time between stirring to 10 seconds. Check that the temperature doesn't rise above 30ºC (86ºF). Repeat until most of the chocolate has melted, but a few lumps are still visible. Stir thoroughly until the chocolate is smooth, thick, and glossy.

3 Pour two-thirds of the chocolate onto the marble or granite. Keep the remaining chocolate warm. Immediately begin to work the chocolate. Using a palette knife and the metal spatula, spread it back and forth across the work surface.

KEEP THE CHOCOLATE MOVING ON THE MARBLE SO IT COOLS AT AN EVEN RATE

4 Keep the chocolate moving constantly to ensure that it cools at an even rate. Continue to work the chocolate for about 2–3 minutes, until the chocolate thickens and cools to 28ºC (82ºF).

5 Add the tempered chocolate into the reserved chocolate and stir. Taking care not to overheat it, place the bowl over a saucepan of simmering water and heat until the chocolate reaches 30ºC (86ºF) and is smooth and glossy. Test the temper (see p151) and use immediately.

MAKING BARS AND SLABS

Making beautifully moulded, professional-looking bars and slabs of chocolate is a lot easier than you'd think. If you've made chocolate from cocoa beans, this is the best way to show off your creation – pure, with nothing to distract from the natural flavours. Use good-quality moulds to ensure the best results (see p139).

WHAT YOU NEED

TIME
15 mins, plus setting

SPECIAL EQUIPMENT
chocolate bar mould
(see p139)

INGREDIENTS
300g (10oz) chocolate,
tempered (see
pp150–53; the exact
quantity depends on
the capacity of your
mould)

MAKES
about 6 small bars

1 Ensure the mould is clean and dry before you begin (see box, below). Use a ladle to carefully fill the mould with tempered chocolate. Start towards the centre of the mould and gently push the chocolate towards the edges using the base of the ladle.

2 If your mould has cavities for multiple bars, repeat this process to fill them all. Firmly tap the mould on the work surface several times to remove remaining air bubbles. Take care to keep the mould level and not to splash the chocolate.

LOOKING AFTER YOUR MOULDS

Before using the moulds for the first time, wash them gently in warm, soapy water. Do not use a scourer, as tiny scratches will show in the chocolate. Dry the moulds thoroughly with a soft cloth before using. Avoid washing the moulds after each use – instead, gently polish the moulds with a tissue, cloth, or a piece of cotton wool. Residual cocoa butter aids the polishing process and gives your chocolate a better shine next time round.

MAKING SLABS

You can make chocolate slabs using plastic containers as moulds: 675g (1½ lb) chocolate makes a 20 x 14cm (8 x 5¾ in) slab that is 2cm (¾ in) deep. For an impressive marbled surface, drizzle a little melted chocolate of a different colour across the slab before it sets, then use a toothpick to draw patterns on the surface.

3 Place the filled mould into the fridge for 20–30 minutes to set. Don't leave the chocolate in the fridge for longer than this, or condensation may form on its surface. When your chocolate is set, it will shrink away from the edges of the mould, allowing it to be removed easily.

4 Place a clean chopping board or baking tray on top of the mould. Clasp the mould and board together firmly with both hands, then turn both over at the same time. The bars should drop out of the mould cleanly, leaving you with beautifully tempered, home-made chocolate.

ADDING FLAVOURS

You can experiment with adding flavour to chocolate once you have tempered it. Stir solid pieces of fruit, nuts, or spices into chocolate before moulding, sprinkle toppings on top of bars in their moulds, or make moreish chunks of chocolate bark. Taste the chocolate in its natural form, and choose ingredients that complement the natural flavours in the chocolate.

MAKING BARK

Chocolate bark is a thin layer of solid chocolate with added toppings – it's simple to make and endlessly customizable. Add splashes of colour with your toppings to make visually impressive barks that make great gifts. Simply spread tempered chocolate out on a baking sheet and sprinkle it with whichever toppings you like (see panel, opposite).

WHAT YOU NEED

TIME
10 mins, plus setting

INGREDIENTS
400g (14oz) dark
  chocolate, tempered
  (see pp150–53)

handful pistachios,
  chopped

handful pecans, chopped

handful dried cranberries

2 tsp sea salt flakes

MAKES
1 large sheet of bark

1 Cover a baking tray with greaseproof paper and use a ladle to pour the tempered chocolate into the centre. Let the chocolate flow to its natural depth. Tap the tray firmly on the work surface to even out the depth of the chocolate and release any air bubbles.

2 Sprinkle the pistachios, pecans, cranberries, and sea salt (or whichever toppings you prefer – see panel, opposite) onto the surface of the chocolate. Work quickly, adding all the toppings before the chocolate starts to set. Refrigerate for 20–30 minutes until the chocolate is just set.

3 Once the chocolate has set, remove it from the fridge and break it into large, irregular shards to serve. Bark can be stored in an airtight container in a cool, dry place for up to 3 months, depending on the shelf life of your chosen toppings.

MIX AND MATCH

Experiment with delicious, visually impressive toppings on dark, milk, and white chocolate. Think about texture and appearance as well as flavour. Crunchy ingredients, such as nuts, crumbled cookies, and broken pretzels, work well with the smooth texture of chocolate. Jewel-like dried fruit and zingy flavourings such as chilli flakes or orange zest add both flavour and colour to chocolate barks, bars, and slabs.

Dark chocolate bark drizzled with white chocolate, with crushed pretzels, chilli flakes, and sea salt

Milk chocolate bark with hazelnuts and raisins

White chocolate bark with chopped, toasted almonds and freeze-dried raspberry pieces

Behind the scenes | Dom Ramsey

THE BEAN-TO-BAR MAKER

Dom Ramsey is a chocolate expert and the founder of Damson Chocolate, a micro-batch bean-to-bar chocolate maker based in London, UK. Ramsey experiments with new flavours and ingredients in his chocolate, and sources beans directly from farmers in areas known for fine flavour, such as Madagascar, Tanzania, and Brazil.

Started his chocolate blog, *Chocablog*, in 2006

Began making bean-to-bar chocolate in 2014

Winner of three Academy of Chocolate awards

Having written about chocolate for more than a decade, Dom Ramsey decided to create his own chocolate in his kitchen. He founded Damson Chocolate in 2015, and now makes fine-quality chocolate in very small batches in a kitchen and shop in North London. Damson Chocolate is going from strength to strength, and was winner of three awards including "The One to Watch" at the 2015 Academy of Chocolate awards.

Ramsey has direct contact with cocoa farmers to source his cocoa beans, and enjoys interacting with customers at the shop. He produces a range of dark chocolate and dark milk chocolate, experimenting with natural ingredients such as buffalo milk powder and Anglesey sea salt.

The future is very bright for Damson Chocolate and an increasing number of other small bean-to-bar chocolate makers in the world, as consumers are asking more questions about sustainability, ethics, and where their food comes from. As the chocolate maker, Ramsey can tell his customers exactly where every ingredient comes from and how it was produced – this ethos is seen by many as the future for the chocolate industry.

CHOCOLATE CHALLENGES
As with many start-up businesses, cashflow is a challenge for Damson Chocolate. Sourcing ingredients, particularly small quantities of good-quality cocoa beans, can be difficult – just one or two standard 65kg (145lb) sacks can last

Ramsey a long time, and most sellers are geared up to deal with buyers who need several tonnes of beans, so Ramsey has needed to build new relationships with farmers and co-operatives.

A DAY IN THE LIFE
Ramsey undertakes varied tasks in the kitchen depending on the current stage of the chocolate-making process – he sorts, roasts, breaks, winnows, and grinds cocoa beans using specialized equipment, creating small samples, tasting, and adjusting recipes for best results.

CUSTOMER FACE-TO-FACE
Ramsey enjoys interacting with customers at the shop and explaining the bean-to-bar process and what makes his chocolate special.

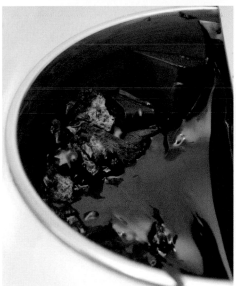

DAMSON VARIETIES
Ramsey encourages customers to try his chocolate in the shop before they buy so they can experience the different flavours and levels of intensity in his selection.

TEMPERING MACHINE
Ramsey uses a rotating-bowl machine to temper his chocolate – this heats and cools chocolate to specific temperatures.

AGEING UNTEMPERED CHOCOLATE
Blocks of chocolate are aged to allow for flavours to develop. The labels indicate specifics about the chocolate – when it was made and the ingredients.

MAKING GANACHE

At the heart of many chocolate recipes is a simple ganache: a mixture of melted chocolate and cream. This recipe makes a ganache suitable for filling chocolates or layering cakes. Once you've mastered this basic technique, experiment with different flavours and textures.

WHAT YOU NEED

TIME
15 mins, plus cooling

INGREDIENTS
200ml (7fl oz) double cream
200g (7oz) good-quality dark chocolate, broken into pieces

MAKES
400g (14oz) ganache

1 Gently heat the cream in a saucepan over a low heat. Do not allow it to come to the boil.

2 Remove the saucepan from the heat and add the chocolate a few pieces at a time. Stir well with a silicone spatula.

VARYING THE RATIO

You can produce ganaches of different textures by varying the amount of cream in the recipe. Softer ganaches are more suitable for sauces, and firmer ganaches can be cut into squares and dipped in tempered chocolate. For a glossy ganache glaze that's perfect for covering cakes, add 20g (¾ oz) unsalted butter along with the chocolate.

3 When the chocolate has completely melted into the cream to create a smooth ganache, transfer it into a bowl.

4 Allow the ganache to cool in the fridge for approximately 1 hour before using it. You can store the ganache, covered, in the fridge for up to 1 week.

ROLLING AND DIPPING TRUFFLES

Envelope pieces of soft ganache in a crisp chocolate shell to create truffles with tempting texture contrast. Roll them by hand and dip them in tempered chocolate to keep the ganache centres fresh for longer. With a little patience – and perhaps a small amount of mess – anyone can master this technique and get professional results.

WHAT YOU NEED

TIME
30 mins, plus chilling and setting

SPECIAL EQUIPMENT
confectioner's dipping tool (optional)

INGREDIENTS
400g (14oz) ganache (see pp160–61), at room temperature
500g (1lb 2oz) good-quality dark chocolate, roughly chopped

MAKES
30–35 truffles

1 Line a baking tray with greaseproof paper. Use two teaspoons to shape roughly walnut-sized balls of ganache, and place them on the baking sheet. Repeat until all the ganache has been used up. Chill for 10 minutes until firm.

2 Remove the truffles from the fridge. One by one, roll each ball in your hand to form consistently sized balls. Work quickly, so that the ganache doesn't melt. Line your truffles on the baking tray and return them to the fridge for a further 15 minutes.

3 Meanwhile, temper your chocolate, as shown on pp150–53, and line another baking tray with greaseproof paper.

4 Remove the balls of ganache from the fridge. Working quickly and efficiently, pick up a truffle, using the dipping tool or an everyday fork, and completely submerge it in the tempered chocolate. A fork will leave marks on the surface of the chocolates, but specialized dipping tools are made from thin wire that doesn't mark melted chocolate.

5 When the ball of ganache is completely covered in chocolate, carefully lift it out and slide the bottom of the dipping tool over the edge of the bowl to remove excess chocolate. Transfer the dipped truffle to the baking tray, gently tilting it to allow it to slide off the tool. Repeat the process with each ball of ganache.

6 Return the truffles to the fridge for up to 15 minutes to set. Do not store them in the fridge, or condensation might spoil the finish. You can store the truffles in an airtight container in a cool, dark place for up to 7 days.

COMPLETELY SUBMERGE TRUFFLES IN TEMPERED CHOCOLATE

MOULDING CHOCOLATES

Filled chocolates are usually the realm of the professional chocolatier, but the chocolate enthusiast can easily master the basics at home. A filled chocolate is simply a chocolate shell filled with a delicious filling – here, the filling is a classic ganache. Mix it up by using a flavoured ganache (see p161).

WHAT YOU NEED

TIME
35 mins, plus
tempering and setting

SPECIAL EQUIPMENT
24-hole chocolate mould
(see p139)

palette knife

2 piping bags

1cm (½ in) plain nozzle

INGREDIENTS
400g (14oz) ganache
(see pp160–61), at room
temperature

300g (10oz) good-quality
dark chocolate,
broken into pieces

MAKES
24 chocolates

1 Temper 250g (9oz) of the chocolate, as per the instructions on pp150–53. Use a ladle to completely fill each of the cavities in the mould with the tempered chocolate. Tap the mould firmly on the work surface to remove any air bubbles.

2 Use a palette knife to scrape away excess chocolate from the top of the mould. Work quickly to avoid the chocolate setting in the mould.

3 Invert the mould to allow the chocolate to flow back into the bowl, leaving a thin layer of chocolate lining each cavity. Scrape any excess chocolate from the top of the mould using the palette knife. Tap the mould firmly on the work surface to even out the level of the chocolate.

4 Give the chocolate a minute or two to set, then turn the mould upside-down onto a baking tray lined with greaseproof paper. Refrigerate the mould for 20 minutes, until the chocolate is completely set.

5 Snip a small hole in the pointed end of one of the piping bags and place the nozzle into the end. Spoon ganache into the bag, pushing it to the pointed end, and twisting the top of the bag closed. Carefully pipe ganache into each cavity, to about 3mm (⅛ in) from the top of the mould.

6 Return the mould to the fridge for 20 minutes to allow the fillings to firm up. Meanwhile, temper the remaining chocolate and use it to fill the second piping bag. Remove the chocolates from the fridge, and top each one with a thin layer of tempered chocolate. Tap the mould firmly on the work surface, and return to the fridge for 20 minutes to set.

7 Once set, turn the chocolates out onto a baking sheet lined with greaseproof paper. The chocolates should fall out cleanly. If any remain, gently tap the mould to dislodge them. You can store the chocolates in an airtight container in a cool, dark place for up to 7 days.

COOKING WITH CHOCOLATE

For off-the-scale flavour, use the best-quality chocolate you can afford in baking and cooking. The right choice can transform the simplest cake or savoury recipe into something spectacular – especially if the dish features ingredients that enhance the flavour profile of the chocolate.

THE RIGHT CHOCOLATE

Despite what you may assume, using "baking chocolate" or "cooking chocolate" does not give you the best results. These products are often made with small percentages of poor-quality cocoa solids, and include very high levels of sugar and other additives. However, fine-quality chocolate is more expensive, so if you are baking regularly, consider using good-quality couverture instead, as it will be cheaper (see box, opposite).

USE CHOCOLATE THAT YOU ENJOY EATING AND IT CAN ENHANCE YOUR RECIPES WITH RICH FLAVOUR

Look at the label

Look at the ingredients list when buying chocolate for your recipe – it should be a short list. Avoid chocolate that includes vegetable fats, such as palm oil, and flavourings or artificial vanilla (vanillin).

INGREDIENTS
Cocoa solids (cocoa mass, cocoa butter), sugar, milk powder, emulsifier (lecithin)

Check the numbers

Make sure that the cocoa-solid percentage is high. If you need dark chocolate for your recipe, choose a bar that has at least 70 per cent cocoa solids, unless the recipe states otherwise. For milk chocolate, choose a variety that contains at least 30 per cent cocoa solids.

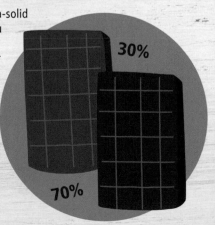

30%

70%

DARK CHOCOLATE
You can soften bitter dark chocolate in light, sweet recipes such as cheesecake or chocolate mousse; it can also be used in intensely flavoured desserts such as flourless chocolate cake.

Taste before you start

It is so important to taste the chocolate before baking with it. The better the chocolate you put in your recipe, the better the finished recipe will taste. If you're using a chocolate that you wouldn't enjoy eating on its own, it's unlikely to enhance your dish.

MILK CHOCOLATE
Opt for good-quality milk chocolate in ice-cream recipes – the complex flavours of dark chocolate are often lost when served cold.

WHITE CHOCOLATE
Match creamy white chocolate with a little dark chocolate in recipes, to offset the sweetness, or pair it with fresh berries: the slight acidity cuts through the richness of the cocoa butter.

Match the flavours

Match the chocolate with the flavours and textures in the recipe. For example, you could choose a naturally fruity Madagascan chocolate for a Black Forest gâteau, or a rich Ecuadorian dark chocolate for a mud cake.

COCOA POWDER
Readily available "natural" cocoa powder is suitable for most recipes, but some specify "Dutch process" cocoa – this has been treated to reduce acidity, giving it a nutty flavour.

ENJOY

Indulge in recipes from the world's finest chocolatiers, pastry chefs, and chocolate experts. Thanks to the ultimate ingredient pairings, these sweet and savoury recipes bring off-the-scale chocolate flavours into the limelight.

Edd Kimber

FLOURLESS CHOCOLATE AND ALMOND BUNDTS

Many flourless cakes are dense and rich, but this recipe has light, fudge-like results. My recipe is definitely one for chocolate lovers – for all-out flavour it combines chocolate and cocoa in the cake, and drizzled chocolate on top.

MAKES 6

WHAT YOU NEED

TIME
25–30 mins

SPECIAL EQUIPMENT
6-hole mini bundt tin

INGREDIENTS
115g (4oz) unsalted butter, diced, plus extra for greasing

1 tsp baking powder

30g (1oz) cocoa powder

115g (4oz) ground almonds

155g (5½oz) good-quality dark chocolate, 60–70% cocoa, chopped

3 large eggs, separated

115g (4oz) caster sugar

1 Preheat the oven to 180°C (350°F/Gas 4). Grease the bundt tin, paying particular attention to the bottom of the moulds and around the central rings. Chill the tin until needed.

2 Combine the baking powder, cocoa powder, and almonds in a bowl and set aside. Heat the butter and 55g (1¾oz) of the chocolate in a small saucepan over a low heat, stirring regularly, until melted and combined. Set aside.

3 Place the egg yolks and half the sugar in a large bowl and beat with a hand-held electric whisk until pale. Gradually pour the chocolate mixture into the egg-yolk mixture and stir together using a silicone spatula until combined. Add the cocoa and almond mixture to the bowl and stir to combine.

4 In a separate large bowl, whisk the egg whites until they form soft peaks. Slowly pour in the remaining sugar, whisking constantly, until the meringue forms glossy, stiff peaks.

5 Add one-third of the meringue mixture to the chocolate batter and gently fold to combine. Repeat with the remaining meringue, adding it in two additions.

6 Divide the mixture equally between the bundt moulds. Bake for 15 minutes until a skewer inserted into the cakes comes out clean. Allow to cool in the tin for 10 minutes before inverting onto a wire rack to cool completely.

7 Melt the remaining chocolate in a heatproof bowl set over a pan of simmering water, stirring until smooth. Do not allow the base of the bowl to touch the water.

8 Serve the cooled bundt cakes with the melted chocolate drizzled over the top. You can store the bundt cakes, without topping, in an airtight container for 2–3 days.

TIP If you're having trouble removing the cakes from the tin, soak a clean tea towel in boiling water, place the cakes in their tin on top of the tea towel, and leave for 5–10 minutes. This should make it easier to invert the cakes onto a wire rack, as per step 6.

Bryan Graham

CHOCOLATE SOUFFLÉS
with peanut gianduja

These soufflés boast a light, cloud-like texture with a surprise peanut filling. Gianduja, a sweet confectionery spread hailing from Turin in Italy, is traditionally made from hazelnuts and milk chocolate. Enjoy my peanut and white chocolate variation, which melts into the rich soufflé mixture.

MAKES 6

WHAT YOU NEED

TIME
1 hr 5 mins–1 hr 25 mins,
  plus chilling

SPECIAL EQUIPMENT
6 x 150ml (5fl oz) ramekins

INGREDIENTS
75g (2½ oz) unsalted butter,
  plus extra for greasing

30g (1oz) plain flour, plus extra
  for dusting

80g (2¾ oz) good-quality dark
  chocolate, 70% cocoa, chopped

3 eggs

75g (2½ oz) caster sugar

double cream, whipped until
  thick, to serve

good-quality dark chocolate
  shavings, 70% cocoa,
  to decorate

For the gianduja
100g (3½ oz) raw, unsalted
  peanuts, skins removed

100g (3½ oz) good-quality white
  chocolate, chopped

1 Preheat the oven to 160°C (325°F/Gas 3). Grease the ramekins, dust them lightly with flour, and set aside.

2 For the gianduja, roast the peanuts for 15–20 minutes until golden in colour. Turn the oven off. Grind the roasted peanuts in a small food processor – they will turn into a fine powder and then gradually form a thick paste. Transfer to a bowl and set aside.

3 Temper the white chocolate (see pp150–53) and add it to the ground peanuts. Stir through until combined. Refrigerate for about 1½ hours, until set. Scoop out teaspoonfuls of the mixture and roll them into even-sized balls using your hands. Place in a bowl, cover, and set aside.

4 Preheat the oven to 160°C (325°F/Gas 3). Place the chopped dark chocolate in a heatproof bowl. Heat the butter in a saucepan over a medium–low heat until simmering. Pour the butter over the chocolate and whisk until the mixture is smooth, with no lumps. Set aside.

5 To make the soufflé mixture, use a hand-held electric whisk on a medium–high setting to whisk the eggs and sugar for 3–4 minutes until pale. Take care not to over-aerate the mixture.

6 Reduce the whisk speed to low and gradually pour the chocolate mixture into the eggs. Whisk until just combined. Gently fold in the flour using a silicone spatula.

7 Place 1 ball of gianduja into each prepared ramekin and pour over the soufflé mix, dividing the mixture evenly between the ramekins. Bake for 12–13 minutes to allow the soufflés to cook and the gianduja to melt completely.

8 Allow the soufflés to rest at room temperature for 1 minute before serving with whipped cream and shavings of dark chocolate.

TIP You could use good-quality, additive-free peanut butter in place of the roasted and blended peanuts in the gianduja. Simply mix 100g (3½ oz) smooth peanut butter with the tempered white chocolate until combined, and refrigerate as per step 2.

Lisabeth Flanagan

MAPLE AND CHOCOLATE FONDANTS with sea salt

Chocolate and maple syrup are a natural pairing for us cold-weather folks in Canada. When making this recipe, I enjoy the view of a large maple tree that sits outside the kitchen window, reminding me of my Canadian roots, and the "roots" of the ingredients in my chocolate creations.

MAKES 8

WHAT YOU NEED

TIME
55 mins–1 hr

SPECIAL EQUIPMENT
8 x 150ml (5fl oz) dariole moulds
  or pudding basins

INGREDIENTS
175g (6oz) unsalted butter,
  plus extra for greasing

115g (4oz) plain flour, plus
  extra for dusting

250g (9oz) good-quality
  dark chocolate, 70% cocoa,
  chopped

350ml (12fl oz) maple syrup

2 eggs, plus 4 egg yolks

1 tsp sea salt flakes

single cream, vanilla ice cream,
  or crème fraîche, to serve

2 tbsp granulated maple sugar,
  to decorate (optional)

For the glaze
115g (4oz) good-quality dark
  chocolate, 70% cocoa, chopped

75ml (2½ fl oz) maple syrup

1 Preheat the oven to 220°C (425°F/Gas 7). Grease the moulds and dust lightly with flour. Melt the chocolate and butter in a heatproof bowl over a small saucepan of gently simmering water. Do not allow the base of the bowl to touch the water. Stir the mixture gently until smooth.

2 Remove the saucepan from the heat, remove the bowl from the bain-marie, and add the maple syrup to the chocolate mixture. Stir until combined. Beat in the eggs and egg yolks until smooth. Stir in the flour and salt.

3 Divide the batter evenly between the moulds, filling them approximately three-quarters full. Place them on a baking sheet, and bake for 12–13 minutes until the cakes are cooked with a still-liquid centre.

4 Meanwhile, for the glaze, melt the chocolate with the maple syrup in a heatproof bowl over a small saucepan of gently simmering water. Do not allow the base of the bowl to touch the water. If the sauce is too thick to pour, add 1–2 teaspoons warm water to the mixture.

5 Turn the baked puddings out onto individual plates. Serve immediately with the glaze drizzled over the top, with single cream, vanilla ice cream, or crème fraîche. Sprinkle with maple sugar, if desired.

Micah Carr-Hill

BAKED DARK CHOCOLATE CHEESECAKE

This rich and creamy cheesecake contains less sugar than usual to bring out the full flavour of the chocolate. I make the base using ginger biscuits – this adds texture and a subtle flavour contrast to the chocolate filling.

SERVES 12–14

WHAT YOU NEED

TIME
1 hr 50 mins, plus cooling and chilling

SPECIAL EQUIPMENT
22cm (9¾ in) springform cake tin

INGREDIENTS
50g (1¾ oz) unsalted butter

200g (7oz) good-quality ginger biscuits (choose ones without added lemon oil)

20g (¾ oz) skimmed milk powder

¾ tsp sea salt

4 tbsp double cream

single cream, lightly whisked, to serve

For the filling
200g (7oz) good-quality dark chocolate, 70% cocoa, chopped

425g (15oz) full-fat cream cheese

135g (4¾ oz) soured cream

4 large eggs

90g (3¼ oz) caster sugar

25g (scant 1oz) cocoa powder, sifted

2 generous pinches of sea salt

½ tsp vanilla extract

1 Preheat the oven to 110°C (225°F/Gas ¼). Melt the butter in a small saucepan over a low heat. Brush a little of the melted butter on the inside of the cake tin and set aside.

2 Blitz the biscuits in a food processor until they have a crumb-like texture. Use 2 tablespoons of the crumbs to dust the sides of the tin, knocking excess crumbs back into the food processor.

3 Add the milk powder and salt to the remaining biscuit crumbs, and pulse briefly to combine. Add the remaining melted butter and the cream and blitz until combined. Use this mixture to line the bottom of the tin, pushing it slightly up the sides. Cover and refrigerate.

4 To make the filling, melt the chocolate in a heatproof bowl over a pan of simmering water, stirring until smooth. Do not allow the base of the bowl to touch the water.

5 Whisk together the cream cheese and soured cream until smooth. In a separate bowl, whisk together the eggs and sugar. Combine the two mixtures.

6 Whisk the melted chocolate into the mixture until combined. Whisk in the sifted cocoa powder. Season with the salt and vanilla extract, taste, and adjust the seasoning if necessary.

7 Remove the cake tin from the fridge and place it on a baking sheet. Pour the filling over the base. Bake for 1 hour 20 minutes.

8 Once cooked, the top of the cheesecake should have only a slight wobble in the centre, without any cracks. Remove from the oven and run a sharp knife around the edge to release it from the sides.

9 Turn the oven off and return the cheesecake to the oven, leaving the door open. This will allow the cheesecake to cool slowly, helping to prevent cracking.

10 Once cool, cover and refrigerate for at least 2 hours or overnight. For clean slices, use a sharp knife dipped in boiling water and wiped dry between each slice. Serve with single cream. You can store the cheesecake, covered, for up to 1 week in the fridge.

SERVES 10–12

WHAT YOU NEED

TIME
1 hr 10 mins, plus steeping
  and cooling

SPECIAL EQUIPMENT
2 x 26cm (10½ in) cake tins

INGREDIENTS
50g (1¾ oz) unsalted butter, plus
  extra for greasing

50g (1¾ oz) plain flour

25g (scant 1oz) cocoa powder

50g (1¾ oz) good-quality
  dark chocolate, 65–70%
  cocoa, chopped

215g (7½ oz) marzipan, grated

65g (2¼ oz) icing sugar

6 eggs, separated

65g (2¼ oz) caster sugar

120g (4¼ oz) good-quality
  apricot jam

1 sheet ready-rolled marzipan

50g (1¾ oz) white chocolate, finely
  chopped

whipped cream, to serve
  (optional)

For the chocolate glaze
120g (4½ oz) dark couverture
  chocolate, finely chopped

115ml (3¾ fl oz) double cream

100g (3½ oz) caster sugar

40g (1½ oz) cocoa powder

Christian Hümbs
SACHERTORTE

Created in 19th-century Vienna, this dark chocolate torte combines nutty marzipan, tart apricot jam, and rich chocolate in an impressive cake. For a perfect, professional-quality glaze, use good-quality couverture, which contains more cocoa butter than normal chocolate bars, lending extra sheen to the topping.

1 Preheat the oven to 180°C (350°F/Gas 4). Grease and line the tins with baking parchment. Mix the flour and cocoa powder in a large bowl. Melt the chocolate and butter together in a heatproof bowl set over a pan of simmering water, stirring until it melts. Do not allow the base of the bowl to touch the water.

2 Place the grated marzipan and icing sugar in a food processor and mix until combined. Gradually add the egg yolks, 2 egg whites, and 65ml (2¼fl oz) cold water, and whisk until smooth.

3 In a separate bowl, whisk the remaining egg whites until soft peaks form. Then add the caster sugar, 1 tablespoon at a time, and whisk after each addition until the mixture is well combined and forms stiff peaks.

4 Fold a little egg white mixture into the marzipan mixture, then fold in a little flour and cocoa mixture, then a little chocolate mixture. Add a little more of each mixture, folding after each addition, until all the mixtures have been combined

5 Divide the mixture evenly between the two tins. Bake in the middle of the oven for 16–17 minutes until just firm to the touch. Remove the sponge from the oven and leave to cool.

6 To make the glaze, place the couverture chocolate in a heatproof bowl. Bring 75ml (2½fl oz) of the cream to the boil and pour over the top. Wait for 30 seconds before stirring with a silicone spatula until combined, thick, and glossy.

7 Dissolve the caster sugar in 250ml (9fl oz) cold water in a saucepan and bring to the boil. Stir in the cocoa powder and bring it back to the boil. Add the remaining cream and bring to the boil again.

8 Remove from the heat, and stir the mixture into the couverture mixture, incorporating as little air as possible. Cover and leave to cool before transferring to the fridge.

9 Warm the jam gently in a pan over a low heat. Remove the cooled sponges from the tins and spread one with half the apricot jam. Place the second sponge on top, and thinly cover the top and sides of the whole cake with the remaining jam.

10 Lift the unrolled marzipan over the top of the cake so that it is centred, and smooth it over the top, pushing out any air bubbles. Press down around the sides of the cake. If there are cracks, pinch it together or patch. Rub it with your fingers until smooth. Trim off the excess marzipan. Place the cake on a wire rack over a baking tray.

11 Warm the chocolate glaze very gently in a heatproof bowl over a pan of simmering water. Do not overheat it. At the same time, melt the white chocolate in a heatproof bowl over a pan of simmering water. Do not allow the base of the bowl to touch the water.

12 Pour the warmed glaze over the cake, a little at a time. Use a palette knife to spread the glaze evenly over the top and sides of the cake. Drizzle thin lines of the melted white chocolate across the top. Working quickly, gently draw a toothpick through the white chocolate to create a feathered effect. Allow to cool, then serve the cake with whipped cream, if desired. You can store the cake in an airtight container for up to 3 days.

TIP Ready-rolled marzipan is available in supermarkets and specialist baking shops. If you can't get hold of it, you can make your own at home. Knead 250g (9oz) cubed marzipan with 125g (4½oz) icing sugar and 1 tbsp rum until combined. Roll the mixture out between baking parchment or cling film to form a disc approximately 5mm (¼in) thick.

Bryan Graham

DARK CHOCOLATE AND STOUT CAKE

Beer and chocolate make a delicious combination when balanced carefully. I've showcased the flavour pairing in this recipe – the bitter tang of stout brings an added dimension to the rich, moist sponge cake.

SERVES 10–12

WHAT YOU NEED

TIME
1 hr 5 mins, plus cooling

SPECIAL EQUIPMENT
2 x 20cm (8in) deep cake tins
mixer with whisk attachment

INGREDIENTS
300g (10oz) unsalted butter,
   plus extra for greasing
330ml (11¾ fl oz) stout
580g (1lb 4¾ oz) caster sugar
270g (9½ oz) plain flour
85g (3oz) cocoa powder
1 tsp baking powder
generous pinch of salt
seeds from 1 vanilla pod
130g (4¾ oz) honey
5 eggs
75g (2½ oz) buttermilk
175g (6oz) good-quality dark
   chocolate, 70% cocoa,
   finely grated
dark chocolate curls, to decorate

For the ganache
340g (11¾ oz) good-quality dark
   chocolate, 70% cocoa, chopped
255g (9¼ oz) double cream
85ml (3fl oz) stout
45g (1½ oz) unsalted butter,
   softened

1 Preheat the oven to 160°C (325°F/Gas 3). Grease and line the tins with baking parchment. Bring 80ml (2¾ fl oz) of the stout to the boil in a small saucepan over a medium heat. Add 80g (2¾ oz) of the sugar and stir until dissolved. Remove the syrup from the heat and leave to cool.

2 Sift the flour, cocoa powder, and baking powder into a bowl. Cream the butter, remaining sugar, salt, and vanilla in the mixer until pale and fluffy. Add the honey, then the eggs, one at a time, pulsing until combined.

3 Add one-third of the flour mixture to the mixer on a low speed until just combined. Gradually add the buttermilk. Add another third of the flour mixture, and then the remaining stout. Mix in the remaining flour mixture until combined. Fold the grated chocolate into the batter.

4 Divide the batter evenly between the 2 cake tins and bake for 50 minutes, or until a toothpick inserted into the middle comes out clean. Remove the sponges from the oven and allow to cool in their tins.

5 While the sponges are cooling, prepare the ganache. Place the chopped chocolate in a medium heatproof bowl. Combine the cream and stout in a saucepan, and bring to a simmer, ensuring that it does not boil.

6 Remove the mixture from the heat and pour it over the chocolate in the bowl. Allow to stand for 1–2 minutes. Add the butter to the bowl and begin stirring the mixture, starting in the middle and moving outwards in small circular motions, until combined. Pour the mixture into the mixer, allow to cool a little, and whisk until spreadable.

7 Remove the cooled sponges from their tins. Brush a generous amount of the stout syrup onto the top of one of the sponges using a palette knife, then spread a few generous spoonfuls of more ganache on top.

8 Layer the second sponge on top of the first, and soak it with syrup. Cover the whole cake very thinly with ganache using a palette knife. Refrigerate for 15 minutes.

9 Remove the cake from the fridge and cover with the remaining ganache. Decorate with chocolate curls and serve. You can cover and store the cake in the fridge for up to 2 days, allowing the cake to return to room temperature before serving.

Christian Hümbs

CHERRY AND CHOCOLATE MOUSSE with balsamic glaze

With layers of a tart cherry purée, velvety chocolate mousse, and nutty crumble, this is a show-stopper of a dessert. To keep the mousse as fluffy and aerated as possible, be gentle when you stir the chocolate into the egg-white mixture.

MAKES 6

WHAT YOU NEED

TIME
20–30 mins, plus chilling
and resting

SPECIAL EQUIPMENT
6 x 150ml (5fl oz) serving glasses
or ramekins

INGREDIENTS
330g (11oz) cherries, fresh or
frozen, pitted

1 tbsp icing sugar

50ml (2fl oz) good-quality
matured balsamic vinegar

90g (3oz) caster sugar

100g (3½ oz) good-quality dark
chocolate, 70% cocoa, chopped

3 egg yolks

185ml (6½ fl oz) double cream

dark chocolate curls, to decorate

For the crumble topping
50g (1¾ oz) unsalted butter

80g (2¾ oz) plain flour

30g (1oz) ground hazelnuts

40g (1½ oz) demerara sugar

20g (¾ oz) vanilla sugar, or
caster sugar mixed with
¼ tsp vanilla extract

1 Blend 100g (3½ oz) of the cherries with the icing sugar in a blender or food processor until smooth. Pour the purée into a sieve over a bowl and leave to drain for 5 minutes. Transfer the purée into a small bowl.

2 To make the glaze, pour the drained cherry juice into a small saucepan over a medium–low heat. Add the vinegar and 2 tablespoons of the caster sugar. Simmer, stirring regularly, until the sugar dissolves. Continue until the glaze reduces by two-thirds and is thick and syrupy, about 10 minutes.

3 Add 1 tablespoon of the glaze to the cherry purée in the bowl and mix well. Set aside. Add 6 whole cherries to the glaze in the pan, and toss until they are coated, then transfer them to a plate. Set aside.

4 Melt the chocolate in a heatproof bowl set over a pan of simmering water, stirring until smooth. Do not allow the base of the bowl to touch the water.

5 Place the egg yolks and remaining caster sugar in a medium bowl. Beat using a hand-held electric whisk until thick, pale, and creamy. In a separate bowl, whisk the cream to form stiff peaks.

6 Using a silicone spatula, stir a little melted chocolate into the egg mixture, then mix in the rest. Add one-third of the cream and stir. Add the remaining cream, little by little, stirring until no streaks appear.

7 Divide the remaining, uncoated cherries between the glasses. Add a spoonful of cherry purée to each, then divide the mousse between the glasses. Chill for 1 hour to set.

8 Preheat the oven to 190°C (375°F/Gas 5). Mix all the crumble ingredients in a food processor until combined. Transfer the mix to a lined baking tray in a thin, even layer. Bake for 10 minutes. Allow the crumble to cool for 2 minutes, then break into small pieces.

9 Remove the mousse from the fridge 10–15 minutes before serving. Top with the crumble, chocolate curls, and glazed cherries. You can keep the mousse, covered in the fridge without toppings, for up to 2 days.

Charlotte Flower
FRESH CORIANDER AND LEMON CHOCOLATES

I love using wild or garden herbs. Fresh coriander, with its bright colour and flavour, is a revelation. I've added lemon to counter the sweetness of white chocolate. The ganache is soft, so perfect for moulded chocolates.

MAKES 24

WHAT YOU NEED

TIME
1½ hrs, plus infusing
   and overnight chilling

SPECIAL EQUIPMENT
24-hole polycarbonate chocolate
   mould (see p139)
digital food thermometer
2 disposable piping bags
small, plain piping nozzle

INGREDIENTS
90ml (3fl oz) double cream
20g (¾oz) fresh coriander leaves
   and stems, roughly chopped
zest of 1 lemon
300g (10oz) good-quality dark
   chocolate, 70% cocoa, chopped
165g (5¾oz) good-quality white
   chocolate, finely grated

1 Warm the cream in a saucepan until just below boiling point, ensuring that it does not boil. Remove the cream from the heat and immediately add the chopped coriander and lemon zest to the pan. Stir, cover, and leave for 1 hour to infuse.

2 Temper 240g (8¾oz) dark chocolate (pp150–53). Use it to line the mould cavities, as per steps 1–4 of Moulding chocolates (pp164–65).

3 Place the white chocolate into a heatproof bowl. Reheat the infused cream over a medium–low heat, stirring with a silicone spatula as you do so, until the cream is just coming to the boil. When the cream starts to bubble a little, remove the pan from the heat and pour the cream through a sieve over the white chocolate in the bowl. Use the back of a spoon to push as much cream through the sieve as possible.

4 Tap the bowl on the work surface to spread the cream over the chocolate. Allow to melt for 30 seconds before beginning to stir the mixture with a balloon whisk. Do not beat the mixture; instead gently stir to slowly combine the ingredients. If lumps remain, use a hairdryer to gently warm the mixture as you stir, using a digital food thermometer to ensure that the mixture does not exceed 31°C (88°F).

5 Continue to stir the mixture until it comes together to form a silky, smooth ganache. Check the temperature – the mixture should be below 30°C (86°F). Work quickly, as the ganache will thicken as it cools.

6 Snip a small hole in the end of a piping bag and place the nozzle into the end. Spoon the ganache into the bag, pushing it to the end and twisting the bag closed. Carefully fill each of the mould cavities with ganache to about 2mm (⅛in) from the top, to allow room for capping. Cover with a sheet of baking parchment and leave overnight to fully set.

7 Temper the remaining chocolate and use it to fill the second piping bag. Cap off each chocolate, tap the mould firmly on your work surface, and refrigerate for 20 minutes until set.

8 Once set, turn the chocolates out onto a baking sheet or plate, and serve. You can store them in an airtight container in a cool, dark place for up to 7 days.

Charlotte Flower

WILD GARLIC TRUFFLES

It may be an unusual flavour combination, but mellow, savoury garlic works beautifully with chocolate. It wakes up your tastebuds – making these truffles a great start to a meal. You can also try coating the truffles in crunchy toasted sesame seeds, rather than cocoa powder.

MAKES 18–20

WHAT YOU NEED

TIME
1¼ hrs, plus infusing
and overnight chilling

SPECIAL EQUIPMENT
disposable food gloves

INGREDIENTS
80ml (2¾ fl oz) double cream

4g (scant ⅛ oz) wild garlic leaves
or ramson (*Allium ursinum*)
leaves, finely chopped

115g (4oz) good-quality milk
chocolate, 35% cocoa,
finely grated

15g (½ oz) salted butter, diced
and softened

200g (7oz) good-quality dark
chocolate, 70% cocoa, chopped

50g (1¾ oz) cocoa powder

1 Warm the cream in a saucepan until just below boiling point, ensuring that it does not boil. Remove the cream from the heat and immediately add the chopped garlic leaves to the pan. Stir, cover, and leave for 1 hour to infuse.

2 Place the milk chocolate in a heatproof bowl. Reheat the infused cream over a medium–low heat, stirring with a silicone spatula as you do so, until the cream is just coming to the boil. When the cream starts to bubble, remove the pan from the heat and pour the cream through a sieve over the milk chocolate. Use the back of a spoon to push as much cream through as possible. Tap the bowl on the work surface.

3 Allow to melt for 30 seconds before beginning to stir the mixture with a balloon whisk. Do not beat the mixture; instead gently stir to slowly combine the ingredients. If lumps remain, use a hairdryer to gently warm the mixture as you stir, using a digital food thermometer to ensure that the mixture does not exceed 33°C (91°F).

4 Once combined and lump-free, add the butter and stir until melted. Continue to stir the mixture gently until it has come together to form a silky, smooth ganache. Leave the ganache to cool, before covering and transferring to the fridge. Leave overnight.

5 Use 2 teaspoons to roughly shape 18–20 ganache balls, and place them on a lined baking sheet. Transfer to the fridge for 10 minutes. Remove the ganache balls from the fridge and allow them to come to room temperature. Roll each ball in your hand to form smooth spheres. Line the truffles on the sheet and return to the fridge for 15 minutes.

6 Remove the balls of ganache from the fridge and allow to reach room temperature. Temper the dark chocolate, as shown on pp150–53. Place the cocoa powder in a bowl, and put on the gloves. Working quickly, spoon a little chocolate into your palm. Pick up a ball with your other hand and move it in the chocolate until fully coated. Place the truffle gently in the cocoa to coat. Transfer the truffle to a clean, lined baking sheet. Repeat with all the truffles. Alternatively, use a confectioner's tool to dip the truffles (see pp162–63).

7 Allow the truffles to set in a cool place before serving. You can store them in an airtight container in a cool, dark place for up to 7 days.

A collection of...
TRUFFLES

Once you have mastered the art of making ganache, rolling truffles, and moulding and tempering chocolate, you can experiment with a whole range of flavour combinations, or invent your own unique variations.

BRIGADEIROS

1 To make this Brazilian speciality, place **one 400g can condensed milk**, **3 tbsp cocoa powder** and **1 tbsp unsalted butter** in a heavy-based pan and bring to the boil, stirring constantly until combined.

2 Reduce to a low heat and continue to cook, stirring constantly for 10–15 minutes, until the mixture is very thick and a spoon dragged across the base of the pan will separate the mixture for a few seconds.

3 Turn the mixture out onto a buttered plate and cool to room temperature. Cover with cling film and chill for at least 4 hours until firm.

4 Lightly grease your hands with a little softened butter and roll the mixture into walnut-sized balls. Roll the balls in **chocolate sprinkles** until completely covered, then serve. Store, covered in the fridge, for up to 5 days.

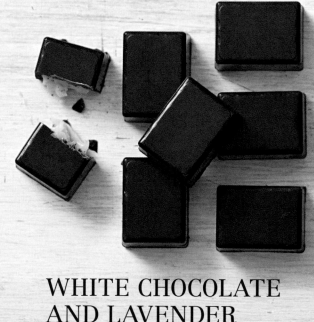

WHITE CHOCOLATE AND LAVENDER

1 Follow the recipe for Fresh coriander and lemon chocolates (see pp184–85). When infusing the cream (in step 1), omit the coriander and lemon and instead add **1 tsp culinary lavender**.

2 Continue with the recipe as described, leaving the chocolates to set before turning them out and serving. You can store the chocolates in an airtight container in a cool, dark place for up to 7 days.

RASPBERRY AND SEA SALT

1 Follow the recipe for Wild garlic truffles (see pp186–87). Omit the garlic from the recipe, and pour the heated cream over the chocolate (step 2).

2 Once you have made the ganache (step 4) stir in **1 tbsp freeze-dried raspberries** and **¼ tsp raspberry extract**. Continue with the recipe.

3 After you have given the truffles their chocolate coating (step 6), omit the cocoa powder dusting and place them on greaseproof paper to set, immediately sprinkling each one with a **little flaky sea salt** as you go.

4 Once set, serve. Store the truffles in an airtight container in a cool, dark place for up to 7 days.

PISTACHIO AND WHITE CHOCOLATE

1 Follow the recipe for Wild garlic truffles (see pp186–87). Omit the garlic from the recipe, just pouring the heated cream over the chocolate (step 2).

2 Once you have made the ganache (step 4), combine a little of it with **1 tbsp pistachio paste**, then mix it all back into the ganache until well combined.

3 Melt **200g (7oz) good-quality white chocolate, finely chopped**, and coat the truffles (step 6). Omit the cocoa powder dusting and place them on greaseproof paper to set, immediately sprinkling each one with **pistachios, finely chopped**.

4 Once set, serve. Store the truffles in an airtight container in a cool, dark place for up to 7 days.

MAKES 14

WHAT YOU NEED

TIME
1 hr 35 mins, plus overnight
 proving and chilling, and resting

SPECIAL EQUIPMENT
mixer with dough hook
 attachment

INGREDIENTS
34g (1¼ oz) fresh yeast or
 3⅓ tsp dried active yeast

315g (10¾ oz) plain flour, plus
 extra for dusting

340g (11¾ oz) strong bread flour

85g (3oz) caster sugar

80g (2¾ oz) dark cocoa powder

½ tsp sea salt

5 eggs, plus 1 egg to glaze

330g (11¾ oz) unsalted butter,
 diced, at room temperature, plus
 extra for greasing

170g (6oz) good-quality
 dark chocolate chips

For the crème pâtissière
2 eggs, plus 6 egg yolks

250g (9oz) caster sugar

1 tsp good-quality vanilla extract

100g (3½ oz) plain flour

900ml (1½ pints) whole milk

140g (5oz) good-quality dark
 chocolate, 70% cocoa, chopped

Bruno Breillet
ALL-CHOCOLATE SWISS BRIOCHE

Brioches Suisses are indulgent breakfast pastries found everywhere in France – strips of light brioche filled with vanilla crème pâtissière and chocolate chips. I'm from Lyon, so I thought I'd give these Swiss brioches the Lyonnais dessert treatment: "if in doubt, add more chocolate"!

1 Dissolve the yeast in 120ml (4fl oz) water at room temperature. If using dried yeast, follow the pack instructions. Place the flours, sugar, cocoa powder, salt, and 5 eggs in a food mixer. Start mixing on a low speed. Gradually add the dissolved yeast to the mixer bowl.

2 Leave the mixer running for 8–10 minutes to form a stiff dough, pausing halfway through to scrape the sides using a silicone spatula. Add the butter a little at a time and mix for 10 minutes. The dough will become stickier and paste-like.

3 Increase the speed to medium for 2 minutes. Scrape the mixture down the sides again and mix on a low speed for 10 minutes until the dough is soft, shiny, and elastic. Transfer the dough to a large greased bowl and loosely cover with cling film. Leave to prove in the fridge overnight.

4 For the crème pâtissière, whisk the eggs and egg yolks in a large bowl. Add the sugar, vanilla, and flour. Whisk vigorously for about 30 seconds until the mixture forms a ribbon when you lift the whisk out.

5 Add half the milk to the mixture, a little at a time, whisking in between additions. Whisk until smooth. Transfer the mixture to a large saucepan, add the remaining milk, and place over a medium heat.

6 Whisk the mixture constantly in a circular motion for 4–5 minutes until the mixture starts to steam. Whisk more vigorously, at a steady pace, to prevent the mixture from curdling. If the mixture begins to bubble or stick to the bottom of the pan, reduce the heat.

7 Continue whisking the mixture until it reaches the consistency of thick custard. Reduce the heat and cook for a further 2 minutes, whisking constantly. Remove from the heat and stir the chocolate into the mixture, using a silicone spatula, until the mixture is fully combined and smooth. Leave for 5 minutes and stir again. Cover with cling film and leave to cool before refrigerating overnight.

8 Remove the dough from the fridge. While the dough is still cold, roll it out on a lightly floured surface into a 35 x 70cm (14 x 28in) rectangle, approximately 5mm (¼ in) thick. With one of the long edges facing you, spread the crème pâtissière over the half of the dough closest to you. Sprinkle the chocolate chips evenly over the crème pâtissière.

9 Fold the uncovered half of the dough over the covered half, very slightly overlapping the side closest to you. Whisk the remaining egg with a little cold water and brush over the top of the folded dough.

10 Cut the length of dough into fourteen 5cm- (2in-) pieces, and transfer them to 2 lined baking sheets. Leave about 1cm (½in) between the pieces. Brush the edges of each brioche with a little of the whisked egg mixture and pinch to seal them. Loosely cover both baking sheets with cling film and leave to rest in a warm place for 1½–2 hours. Preheat the oven to 180°C (350°F/Gas 4).

11 Bake the brioches for 25–35 minutes until risen and the edges start to darken in colour. The dough will be firm to touch.

12 Remove the brioches from the oven and allow them to cool completely. The brioches are best served fresh, but you can store them in an airtight container at room temperature for up to 3 days. You can freeze uncooked brioches for up to 1 month, and baked brioches for up to 2 weeks.

Bill McCarrick

PROFITEROLES with Chantilly cream

These profiteroles are golden, light, and oozing with thick Chantilly cream. Choose an intense dark chocolate to contrast with the light choux buns. Once the buns are cooked, be sure to prick them to allow the steam to escape – this ensures a crisp, delicate pastry.

MAKES 24

WHAT YOU NEED

TIME
45 mins, plus cooling

SPECIAL EQUIPMENT
piping bag fitted with a 5mm
(¼ in) star nozzle

INGREDIENTS
70g (2¼ oz) strong white flour

150ml (5fl oz) whole milk

70g (2¼ oz) salted butter

3 eggs

For the Chantilly cream
200ml (7fl oz) whipping cream

30g (1oz) icing sugar

1 tbsp vanilla extract

For the chocolate sauce
90ml (3fl oz) whole milk

90g (3¼ oz) good-quality dark
chocolate, at least 70% cocoa,
roughly chopped

30g (1oz) unsalted butter,
softened

1 Preheat the oven to 190°C (375°F/Gas 5). Line a large baking sheet with baking parchment. Sift the flour into a large bowl, holding the sieve high to help aerate it.

2 Heat the milk and salted butter in a medium saucepan over a medium heat until just starting to boil. Add the flour to the pan and bring to the boil, stirring constantly with a wooden spoon.

3 After 1 minute, remove the pan from the heat and transfer the mixture into a heatproof bowl. Whisk the mixture with a hand-held electric whisk on a medium speed for 2 minutes.

4 Gradually add the eggs to the mixture, while the whisk is running. Scrape down the sides of the bowl using a silicone spatula to avoid lumps forming.

5 Whisk until all the eggs have been added and the mixture is fully combined. Scoop 24 walnut-sized balls of the batter onto the prepared sheet. Bake for 15–20 minutes, until risen, golden, and crisp.

6 Remove the choux buns from the oven, prick each one in the side, and return them to the oven for a further 5 minutes. Allow them to cool completely on a wire rack. Once cool, use a knife to make a small hole in the side of each bun.

7 For the Chantilly cream, whisk the cream, icing sugar, and vanilla extract together in a large bowl until the mixture forms soft peaks. Set aside.

8 For the chocolate sauce, gently heat the milk in a saucepan, before adding the dark chocolate and butter. Stir over a medium–low heat until combined.

9 Spoon the Chantilly cream into the piping bag and pipe it into the buns. Serve immediately with the chocolate sauce poured over the top.

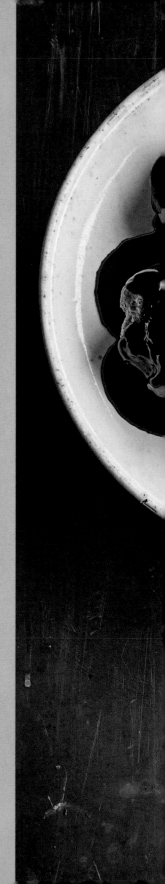

MORE TO TRY

WHITE CHOCOLATE ÉCLAIRS
• Makes 12

Follow the choux recipe opposite, but instead of forming the batter into balls, pipe twelve 10 x 3cm (4 x 1¼ in) lengths of the mixture onto a lined baking sheet. Bake as per the recipe, opposite. To make the filling, fold **150g (5½ oz) sweetened chestnut purée** into **150ml (5fl oz) whipped double cream**. Split the cooled éclairs lengthways and pipe the cream mixture into the centre. Melt **115g (4oz) white chocolate, chopped**, in a heatproof bowl over simmering water, transfer to a piping bag, and cool. Pipe the chocolate in a zigzag over the top of the éclairs. Chill until set. Serve.

CHOCOLATE DULCE DE LECHE PROFITEROLES
• Makes 24

Follow the choux recipe opposite, substituting 15g (½ oz) flour with **15g (½ oz) cocoa powder**. Bake as per the recipe, opposite. To make the filling, whisk **150ml (5fl oz) double cream**. Mix a little of the whipped cream into **150g (5½ oz) dulce de leche**, then fold in the rest. Make a small hole in the base of the buns and pipe the filling into each one. Top with the chocolate sauce, opposite, and serve.

DARK CHOCOLATE AND PISTACHIO ICE CREAM PROFITEROLES
• Makes 24

Follow the method for chocolate choux above. Once the buns are cool, split and fill each one with **1 scoop of pistachio ice cream** and place them in the freezer. To make the ganache, heat **90ml (3¼ fl oz) double cream** and stir in **90g (3¼ oz) dark chocolate, chopped**. Serve frozen, with the warm ganache poured over and **pistachios, finely chopped**, sprinkled on top.

MAKES 30

WHAT YOU NEED

TIME
55 mins, plus resting
and cooling

SPECIAL EQUIPMENT
mixer with whisk attachment
(optional)

2 disposable piping bags, 1 fitted
with a 9mm (⅓ in) round nozzle

INGREDIENTS
160g (5¾ oz) ground almonds

160g (5¾ oz) icing sugar

25g (scant 1oz) Dutch process
cocoa powder (see p167)

140g (5oz) egg whites
(approximately 4 medium egg
whites), at room temperature

180g (6¼ oz) caster sugar

½ tsp brown food colouring paste
(optional)

For the ganache
90ml (3fl oz) red wine

200g (7oz) good-quality dark
chocolate, 70% cocoa,
finely grated

200ml (7fl oz) double cream

1 tsp honey

Bruno Breillet

CHOCOLATE MACARONS
with red wine ganache

This recipe is inspired by memories of Sunday lunches at my parents' house, when guests would bring cakes, flowers, or chocolate and red wine. It is essential to give the almonds a grind in the food processor with the icing sugar, to make sure your macarons have a smooth finish.

1 Use a 3cm (1in) round object to trace 30 circles, 1cm (½ in) apart, on 2 sheets of baking parchment. Turn the sheets over and place them on 2 large baking sheets.

2 Add the ground almonds and icing sugar to a food processor and mix for 2 minutes. Add the cocoa powder and pulse to combine until the mixture is a uniform brown colour. Set aside.

3 Add the egg whites and caster sugar to the mixer, if using, and whisk on a low setting for 3 minutes until combined. Increase the speed to medium and continue to whisk for up to 10 minutes, until the egg whites form stiff peaks. If using a hand-held electric whisk, use the lowest possible setting until the egg whites reach the correct texture.

4 Gently fold the flour mixture and food colouring, if using, into the egg mixture until combined. Do not over-mix: the batter should be firm and slightly deflated. Test the texture by taking a spoonful of the batter and dropping it into the bowl – it should disintegrate within 1 minute.

5 Spoon the batter into the piping bag fitted with the nozzle. Using the traced lines, pipe 30 meringues onto each prepared baking sheet. Tap the baking sheets firmly on the work surface a few times. Set aside until the meringues develop a skin that doesn't stick to your finger when you poke it gently (about 45 minutes).

6 Preheat the oven to 150°C (300°F/Gas 2). Bake the meringues, one sheet at a time, for 13–14 minutes until firm to the touch. Allow both batches to cool on the baking sheets.

7 Meanwhile, prepare the ganache. Boil the red wine in a saucepan over a medium–high heat until reduced by two-thirds. Set aside to cool.

8 Place the chocolate in a heatproof bowl. Heat the cream and honey in a saucepan to just below boiling, ensuring that they do not boil. Pour the cream mixture and the cooled red wine over the chocolate. Stir with a silicone spatula until shiny. Leave to cool until just slightly warm. Transfer to the remaining piping bag and leave to cool further until just set.

9 Cut the tip off the piping bag. Pipe the ganache onto the flat underside of one meringue and sandwich it together gently with the base of a second meringue. Take care not to overfill the macarons, otherwise ganache with spill out of the sides. Repeat until you have sandwiched all the meringues.

10 Leave to rest for at least 2 hours – the flavours will be even better if you leave them until the following day. Serve at room temperature. You can store the macarons in an airtight container in a cool, dark place for up to 5 days.

Lisabeth Flanagan
BLUEBERRY AND WHITE CHOCOLATE TARTLETS

Pairing a very intense dark chocolate pastry with a filling of tangy blueberry and sweet white chocolate, these tartlets provide a delicious contrast in texture, flavour, and colour. They are also very easy to make in advance.

MAKES 8

WHAT YOU NEED

TIME
1–1¾ hrs, plus chilling

SPECIAL EQUIPMENT
8 x 8–10cm (3–3½ in) tartlet tins

baking beans

INGREDIENTS
350g (12oz) unsalted butter,
  chilled and diced, plus extra
  for greasing

225g (8oz) plain flour, plus extra
  for dusting

150g (5½ oz) cocoa powder

85g (3oz) granulated sugar

1 egg, beaten

3 eggs yolks, beaten

blueberries, to decorate

60g (2oz) each good-quality dark
  and white chocolate, tempered
  (see pp150–53), to decorate

For the blueberry filling
350g (12oz) blueberries, fresh
  or frozen

175g (6oz) caster sugar

juice of 1 lemon

For the ganache
450g (1lb) white chocolate,
  finely grated

175ml (6fl oz) whipping cream

2 tbsp unsalted butter, softened

1 Preheat the oven to 180°C (350°F/Gas 4). Grease the tins and dust lightly with flour. Combine the flour, cocoa powder, and granulated sugar in a large bowl. Stir in the butter until the mixture resembles fine breadcrumbs. Add the beaten egg and egg yolks and bring together to form a dough.

2 On a lightly floured surface, roll the dough into a flat, thin rectangle about 3mm (⅛ in) thick. Using a bowl or plate about 5cm (2in) wider in diameter than your tins, cut 10 circles out of the dough.

3 Carefully line each tin with a circle of dough. Trim away excess pastry. Line the pastry cases with greaseproof paper, fill them with baking beans, and place on a baking sheet. Bake for 15–17 minutes, until the dough is cooked through and slightly hardened. Remove from the oven, remove the beans and paper from the cases, and leave to cool.

4 Meanwhile, make the filling. Place the blueberries, sugar, and lemon juice in a saucepan over a medium–high heat. Simmer for 15 minutes. Remove the pan from the heat and allow the mixture to cool. Drain off excess liquid, as this can damage the pastry cases. Set aside.

5 For the ganache, place the white chocolate into a heatproof bowl. Warm the cream in a saucepan until just below boiling point. Pour half the heated cream over the pieces of chocolate in the bowl.

6 Stir the mixture slowly using a silicone spatula. Once the chocolate begins to melt, add the remaining cream. Stir the mixture until smooth. Add the butter and stir to combine. Set aside.

7 Turn the cooled pastry cases out of their tins onto a lined baking sheet. Spread 1 tablespoon of blueberry mixture across the base of each case. Gently reheat the white chocolate ganache in the bowl over a saucepan of simmering water. Divide the softened ganache evenly between the pastry cases. Refrigerate the tartlets for 2 hours until set.

8 Serve the tartlets at room temperature, topped with fresh blueberries and drizzles of tempered dark and white chocolate. You can store the tartlets in an airtight container in the fridge for up to 1 week, or freeze for up to 2 months.

Caroline Bretherton

WHITE CHOCOLATE AND PECAN BLONDIES

Sweet white chocolate, rich in cocoa butter, forms the basis of these delicious blondies. The chopped pecans add texture and crunch – if you prefer, you could also try the same quantity of hazelnuts or pistachios.

MAKES 24

WHAT YOU NEED

TIME
55 mins, plus cooling

SPECIAL EQUIPMENT
20 x 30cm (8 x 12in) baking tin

INGREDIENTS
125g (4½ oz) unsalted butter, plus extra for greasing

275g (9¾ oz) light brown sugar

1½ tsp vanilla extract

3 large eggs

200g (7oz) plain flour

½ tsp sea salt

1 tsp baking powder

125g (4½ oz) pecans, chopped

125g (4½ oz) good-quality white chocolate, finely chopped

1 Preheat the oven to 180°C (350°F/Gas 4). Grease and line the baking tin with baking parchment, leaving some overhang. Melt the butter in a medium saucepan over a gentle heat.

2 Remove from the heat and add the light brown sugar and vanilla extract. Whisk until combined. Add the eggs, one at a time, and whisk well after each addition until the mixture is smooth.

3 Combine the flour, salt, and baking powder in a separate bowl and fold into the mixture until combined. Then use a silicone spatula to fold in the chopped pecans and white chocolate, mixing until evenly combined. Pour the mixture into the tin in an even layer.

4 Bake for 30 minutes until golden brown. Leave to cool slightly in the tin, then remove and peel off the baking parchment. Cut the cake into 24 even-sized pieces and serve warm. You can store them in an airtight container for up to 4 days.

VARIATION To make chocolate brownies, preheat the oven to 160°C (325°F/Gas 3) and grease and line the baking tin. Melt 200g (7oz) chopped good-quality dark chocolate (60% cocoa), with 175g (6oz) unsalted butter in a heatproof bowl over a pan of gently simmering water. Allow to cool slightly before adding 200g (7oz) caster sugar, 125g (4½ oz) soft light brown sugar, and 1 tsp vanilla extract. Beat well to combine. Add 3 eggs, one at a time, beating after each addition. Sift in 125g (4½ oz) plain flour and 1 tsp instant coffee powder and fold gently until well combined. Pour into the prepared tin and bake in the centre of the oven for 45 minutes until just cooked and a skewer inserted into the centre comes out with a little mixture still on it. Allow the cake to cool completely in the tin before turning it out and cutting into 24 pieces.

Paul A. Young

BROWNIE PUDDING with sea-salted caramel, tea, and figs

This sticky-toffee-brownie pudding hybrid is the ultimate comfort food. It incorporates my award-winning sea-salted caramel, along with chocolate, figs, and tea. If you want to make this the day before, brush the top of the pudding with warm caramel as soon as it comes out of the oven, for a sticky toffee glaze.

SERVES 10–12

WHAT YOU NEED

TIME
50–55 mins

SPECIAL EQUIPMENT
20 x 25cm (8 x 10in) cake tin

INGREDIENTS
90g (3¼oz) unsalted butter, softened, plus extra for greasing

180g (6¼oz) self-raising flour, plus extra for dusting

250ml (9fl oz) strong English breakfast tea

1 tsp bicarbonate of soda

200g (7oz) dried figs, chopped

90g (3¼oz) dark muscovado sugar

90g (3¼oz) golden syrup

2 medium eggs

½ tsp sea salt flakes

150g (5½oz) good-quality dark chocolate, 70% cocoa, chopped

roasted cocoa nibs, to decorate (optional)

clotted cream, to serve

For the sauce
200g (7oz) unsalted butter

200g (7oz) dark muscovado sugar

1 tsp sea salt flakes

200ml (7fl oz) double cream

50g (1¾oz) dark milk chocolate, 60% cocoa, chopped

1 Preheat the oven to 180°C (350°F/Gas 4). Grease the tin, dust lightly with flour, and set aside. Combine the tea, bicarbonate of soda, and figs in a medium saucepan over a medium heat. Bring to the boil, and then immediately reduce the heat. Simmer for 2 minutes.

2 Remove the pan from the heat and allow the mixture to cool. Once cooled, mix well with a wooden spoon, until the pieces of fig break down and the mixture forms a paste.

3 In a large bowl, cream together the butter, sugar, and golden syrup, using a wooden spoon. Add the eggs and whisk together until the mixture is smooth. Mix in the flour and salt until combined.

4 Melt the dark chocolate in a heatproof bowl set over a pan of simmering water, stirring until smooth. Do not allow the base of the bowl to touch the water. Add the melted chocolate to the flour mixture, along with the fig paste, and mix well.

5 Pour the batter into the prepared tin. Bake for 30–35 minutes until the pudding has risen and the middle is still slightly gooey.

6 Meanwhile, prepare the sauce. Melt the butter, sugar, and salt in a small saucepan over a medium heat, stirring well to combine. Simmer for 5 minutes. Remove from the heat and add the double cream and dark milk chocolate, whisking well to combine.

7 When ready to serve, cut the pudding into 10–12 pieces and plate them up individually. Pour over the warm sauce, decorate with cocoa nibs, if using, and serve with clotted cream. You can store the pudding, covered in the fridge, for up to 5 days, or freeze it for up to 3 months.

TIP If dark milk chocolate isn't available, use good-quality dark chocolate.

Bill McCarrick

PIANO KEY COOKIES

With delicate layers of lemon and chocolate biscuit, these beautiful cookies melt in the mouth. They may seem intricate, but you can get impressive results from a simple dough using this layer, slice, and freeze method.

MAKES 30

WHAT YOU NEED

TIME
1¼ hrs, plus chilling and freezing

INGREDIENTS
2 egg whites, beaten

For the white dough
240g (8½ oz) plain flour, plus extra
    for dusting

65g (2¼ oz) icing sugar

pinch of sea salt

200g (7oz) unsalted butter, cold

zest of 1 lemon and juice of
    ½ lemon

2 tsp vanilla extract

For the chocolate dough
190g (6¾ oz) plain flour

50g (1¾ oz) cocoa powder

200g (7oz) unsalted butter, cold

65g (2¼ oz) icing sugar

1 To make the white dough, sift the dry ingredients into a mixing bowl. Beat the butter and lemon juice in a food processor until light and creamy. Add the dry ingredients to the processor, along with the lemon zest and vanilla extract. Pulse the mixture until a dough forms. Remove from the processor, wrap in cling film, and chill.

2 To make the chocolate dough, sift the flour and cocoa powder into a mixing bowl. Beat the butter and icing sugar in the processor until light and creamy. Add the flour and cocoa powder and pulse until a dough forms. Remove from the processor, wrap in cling film, and chill.

3 On a lightly floured surface, knead the white dough for 5–10 minutes until smooth. Form into a flat rectangle using your hands. Place the dough between 2 large sheets of baking parchment and roll into a large rectangle about 3–5mm (⅛–¼ in) thick. Remove the top layer of parchment and lift the dough, with the parchment beneath, onto a baking sheet. Brush the top of the dough with the beaten egg white.

4 Knead and roll out the chocolate dough in the same way, and place it on top of the white dough. Use a knife to neaten and trim the edges so that the 2 layers are the same size. Brush the top of the chocolate layer with the egg whites, and place the dough in the freezer for 1 hour.

5 Remove the dough from the freezer. Use a large, sharp knife to cut the dough in half lengthways. Brush the top of one half with egg, and carefully layer the other half on top, so that the colours alternate.

6 Cut the dough in half lengthways again, brush the top of one layer with egg wash, and place the other half on top. You should now have a long, thin strip of 8 layers of dough in alternating colours. Place in the freezer for 1 hour.

7 Remove the dough from the freezer. Cut vertical slices lengthways through the layers, about 3–5mm (⅛–¼ in) thick. Then, cut these long strips into 4cm (1½in) square cookies. Place on a lined baking sheet. Preheat the oven to 180°C (350°F/Gas 4) and allow the cookies to come to room temperature.

8 Bake the cookies for 12–15 minutes until just turning golden brown. Once cooked, allow the cookies to cool completely before removing them from the baking sheet. You can store the cookies in an airtight container at room temperature for up to 5 days.

Micah Carr-Hill

DUCK RAGU with 100 per cent chocolate

Adding port and chocolate to this ragu adds richness and depth of flavour, as well as a little fruitiness. Port and chocolate have a great affinity – the sweetness and fruit flavours of the wine complement the bitterness and fruitiness of the 100 per cent chocolate.

SERVES 6–8

WHAT YOU NEED

TIME
3 hrs 40 mins

SPECIAL EQUIPMENT
meat needle
large flameproof casserole dish

INGREDIENTS
1 whole duck, approximately
 1.2kg (1¾ lb), with giblets
 (if available)

50g (1¾ oz) unsalted butter

sea salt and freshly ground pepper

2 large onions, finely chopped

3 celery stalks, finely chopped

4 large carrots, finely chopped

375ml (13fl oz) white wine

300ml (10fl oz) whole milk

nutmeg, freshly grated

400g can plum tomatoes

35g (1¼ oz) dark chocolate,
 100% cocoa, roughly chopped

3 tbsp good-quality port

flat-leaf parsley, roughly chopped,
 to garnish

1 Preheat the oven to 130°C (250°F/Gas ½). Prick the duck all over with the needle. Melt the butter in the casserole over a medium heat. Add the duck to the pan, with the giblets, if available, and season. Brown the duck all over. Remove to a plate, reserving the fat.

2 Add the onions to the casserole and fry in the residual duck fat. Add the celery and carrots, and fry until softened and lightly browned. Meanwhile, heat the white wine in a saucepan over a medium–high heat, until reduced by two-thirds, to approximately 125ml (4fl oz).

3 Once the vegetables have softened, add the milk and a sprinkle of nutmeg to the casserole. Simmer, stirring occasionally, until the milk has almost evaporated. Add the reduced wine, then crush the tomatoes over the casserole using your hands. Stir to combine and season to taste.

4 Place the duck, breast-side up, on top of the vegetables, and put the lid on. Place in the oven. After 1 hour, turn the duck over. After another hour, turn the duck breast-side up again.

5 After another hour, check to see if the duck is cooked by pulling away a leg – it should come away easily. If not, return to the oven for 10 minutes before retesting. Once cooked, remove from the oven and allow the ragu to cool until the duck is cold enough to handle.

6 Shred the duck meat and add it back into the casserole. The meat should come away from the carcass easily, due to the long cooking time. If using giblets, chop these up, shred the neck meat, and add back into the casserole.

7 Give the casserole a good stir and add 150–300ml (5–10fl oz) boiling water to loosen the ragu. Skim off any excess fat from the surface of the sauce. Check for seasoning.

8 Gradually add the chocolate, one piece at a time, allowing it to melt into the ragu. Taste after each piece, judging the change in flavour and whether to add more or less according to taste. Finally, add the port and stir to combine. Serve with pasta, rice, courgetti, potatoes (baked, sautéed, or mashed), or a green salad.

Maricel E. Presilla

COURGETTES IN CUBAN-STYLE TOMATO SOFRITO
with cacao–almond picada

Adding cocoa nibs to the picada lends texture, depth, and backbone to this dish. Choose a dark chocolate with herbal, grassy undertones for the picada – this will accentuate the fresh flavours of the vegetables.

SERVES 4

WHAT YOU NEED

TIME
40 mins

INGREDIENTS

3 tbsp extra-virgin olive oil

3–4 garlic cloves, crushed

1 medium onion, thinly sliced

225g (8oz) cherry tomatoes, coarsely chopped

½ tsp ground cumin

1 tbsp fresh oregano leaves

¼ tsp ground cayenne pepper

pinch of allspice

1 tsp sea salt

4 medium courgettes, cut into 1cm (½ in) cubes

240ml (8fl oz) warm water or chicken stock

For the picada

30g (1oz) roasted cocoa nibs

12 blanched almonds, lightly toasted

60g (2oz) good-quality dark chocolate, 70–80% cocoa, finely chopped

1–2 garlic cloves, peeled

large handful flat-leaf parsley, finely chopped, plus extra to garnish

1 Heat the oil in a heavy-based frying pan over a medium heat. Add the garlic and fry for 10 seconds. Add the onion and fry, stirring regularly, for 4 minutes.

2 Add the tomatoes, cumin, oregano, cayenne, allspice, and salt to the pan. Stir well to mix, and simmer for 3 minutes.

3 Add the courgettes and cook for a further 2 minutes. Meanwhile, crush the ingredients for the picada together using a large mortar and pestle or food processor, until they form a coarse paste.

4 Add the picada into the tomato mixture, along with the warm water or stock, and stir to combine. Return to the boil, then lower the heat and cover.

5 Simmer for 5 minutes. Season to taste. Serve hot, stirred through rice or spooned over shredded cabbage, drizzled with a little olive oil and sprinkled with salt, to taste.

Maricel E. Presilla

GUATEMALAN-SPICED CACAO DRINK

This version of a traditional Guatemalan drink is a light, non-dairy alternative to hot chocolate. You can drink it as it is, with little pieces of spice and cocoa, or strain it through a fine mesh sieve for a smooth, velvety drink.

SERVES 3–4

WHAT YOU NEED

TIME
20 mins

SPECIAL EQUIPMENT
spice or coffee grinder,
 or small food processor

INGREDIENTS
85g (3oz) cocoa nibs

4 whole allspice berries

2 cinnamon sticks

¼ tsp black peppercorns

100g (3½ oz) brown loaf sugar
 or muscovado sugar

1 Heat a medium, heavy-bottomed frying pan over a medium heat. Add the cocoa nibs and dry-fry for a few seconds until fragrant. Transfer to a bowl.

2 Add the allspice, cinnamon sticks, and peppercorns to the pan and toast lightly for a few seconds until fragrant. Remove from the pan and grind to a fine powder in the grinder.

3 Add the ground spices to the toasted cocoa nibs. Stir to combine, and continue to grind the mixture together until you achieve a fine consistency – you'll need to do this in 2–3 batches.

4 Heat 1 litre (1¾ pints) water in a medium saucepan over a high heat. Add the sugar and stir to dissolve. Bring to the boil. Reduce the heat and add the ground cocoa–spice mixture.

5 Whisk vigorously to combine. You can transfer the mixture to a blender to help to create a creamy texture, if desired. If preferred, strain through a tea strainer or small sieve. Serve hot.

MORE TO TRY

CREAMY HOT CHOCOLATE

- Serves 1

Vary the cocoa percentage of the chocolate according to your individual preference. Combine **250ml (9fl oz) whole milk**, **1 tbsp cocoa powder**, and **50g (1¾oz) good-quality dark chocolate, finely chopped**, with **1 tbsp double cream** and **1 tsp caster sugar** in a small, heavy-based saucepan. Bring to the boil over a medium heat, whisking constantly. Serve.

SPANISH HOT CHOCOLATE

- Serves 1

Place **1 tsp cornflour** and **1 tsp cocoa powder** in a small, heavy-based saucepan. Measure out **250ml (9fl oz) whole milk** and whisk a little into the cornflour mix to make a smooth paste. Add the rest of the milk, along with **50g (1¾oz) good-quality milk chocolate, finely chopped**, and bring to the boil over a medium heat, whisking constantly until smooth. Once it bubbles, reduce to a low simmer and cook for a further 2–3 minutes, whisking occasionally. Serve.

MEXICAN HOT CHOCOLATE

- Serves 1

Combine **250ml (9fl oz) whole milk**, **1 tbsp cocoa powder**, and **50g (1¾oz) good-quality dark chocolate, finely chopped**, with **1 tsp caster sugar**, **¼ tsp vanilla extract**, **¼ tsp ground cinnamon**, and a **pinch of chilli powder** in a small, heavy-based saucepan. Bring to the boil over a medium heat, whisking constantly. Taste and add a little more chilli powder if desired. Once it bubbles, reduce to a low simmer and cook for a further 2–3 minutes, whisking occasionally. Serve.

A collection of...
FONDUES

Smooth and rich, fondue is the simplest way to enjoy chocolate as a dessert. The "dippers" are almost as important as the fondue – use fruit, or try small slices of firm cake, biscotti, or pretzels. Prepare your toppers and skewers before you start making the fondue, as it comes together very quickly. All of these recipes serve 4 people.

DARK CHOCOLATE

1 Finely chop **175g (6oz) good-quality dark chocolate (60% cocoa)**. Place it into a medium heavy-based saucepan, with **125ml (4½ fl oz) whipping cream, 1 tbsp unsalted butter, 1 tbsp caster sugar**, and a **pinch of salt**.

2 Heat the mixture slowly over a medium heat, stirring constantly, until the chocolate has melted and the mixture is smooth, glossy, and warm.

3 Transfer to a fondue set to keep warm, or serve immediately in a bowl with dippers alongside.

WHITE CHOCOLATE AND COCONUT

1 Finely chop **250g (9oz) good-quality white chocolate**. Place it into a medium heavy-based saucepan, along with **125ml (4½ fl oz) whipping cream** and **1 tbsp coconut-flavoured liqueur**.

2 Heat the mixture slowly over a medium heat, stirring constantly, until the chocolate has melted and the mixture is smooth, glossy and warm.

3 Transfer to a fondue set to keep warm, or serve immediately in a bowl with the dippers alongside.

MINI S'MORES

1 Finely chop **240g (8oz) good-quality milk chocolate**. Place it into a medium heavy-based saucepan with **160ml (5½ fl oz) whipping cream**.

2 Heat the mixture slowly over a medium heat, stirring constantly, until the chocolate has melted and the mixture is smooth, glossy, and warm.

3 Divide the mixture evenly between **4 heatproof ramekins**. Gently place small marshmallows on the surface of each fondue, in concentric circles, so that they are entirely covered.

4 Place the ramekins on a baking sheet and grill under a high heat for 1–2 minutes until the marshmallows are well browned (watch them carefully). Serve each bowl with dippers alongside.

CHOCOLATE AND PEANUT BUTTER

1 FInely chop **75g (2½ oz) good-quality dark chocolate (60% cocoa)**. Place it into a medium heavy-based saucepan, along with **150ml whipping cream** and **75g (2½ oz) smooth peanut butter**.

2 Heat the mixture slowly over a medium heat, stirring constantly, until the chocolate has melted and the mixture is smooth, glossy, and warm.

3 Transfer to a fondue set to keep warm, or serve immediately in a bowl with the dippers alongside.

Paul A. Young
STEM GINGER AND FENNEL ICE CREAM

I've found that the palate cannot appreciate the complex flavours of dark chocolate when it is used cold in ice cream. I experimented with milk chocolate, and was blown away by how well its flavours worked served super-cold.

SERVES 6

WHAT YOU NEED

TIME
20 mins, plus cooling, churning, and overnight freezing

SPECIAL EQUIPMENT
ice-cream maker

2.5 litre (4⅓ pint) shallow, freezer-proof lidded airtight container

INGREDIENTS
6 egg yolks

100g (3½ oz) unrefined golden caster sugar

250ml (9fl oz) whole milk

250ml (9fl oz) double cream

75g (2½ oz) good-quality milk chocolate, 40% cocoa, chopped

50g (1¾ oz) crystallized stem ginger

20g (¾ oz) fennel seeds, roughly chopped

1 Prepare the ice-cream maker as per the instructions. In a large bowl, whisk together the egg yolks and sugar until smooth. In a medium saucepan over a medium heat, bring the milk and cream to a simmer.

2 Transfer the milk and cream mixture into a heatproof jug and pour into the egg mixture in a thin stream, whisking well. Once combined, strain the mixture back into the saucepan using a sieve.

3 Cook the mixture over a medium–low heat for 2–3 minutes, stirring constantly, until it is thick enough to coat the back of a spoon.

4 Remove the pan from the heat and add the chocolate, whisking well until combined. Leave to cool completely.

5 Pour the cooled mixture into the ice-cream maker and churn until thick. Meanwhile, chop the ginger into small pieces and combine with the fennel seeds.

6 Once the ice cream is ready, mix in the ginger and fennel seeds, transfer to an airtight container, and freeze overnight. Remove from the freezer 20 minutes before serving. You can store the ice cream for 1–2 months in the freezer.

Dom Ramsey

CHOCOLATE AND HONEY SORBET

This sorbet has all the flavour and texture of a creamy chocolate ice cream, but it has the benefit of being completely dairy-free and – provided you have access to an ice-cream maker – it is incredibly easy to make.

SERVES 4–6

WHAT YOU NEED

TIME
20–25 mins, plus cooling, chilling, and freezing

SPECIAL EQUIPMENT
ice-cream maker

1.5 litre (2¾ pint) shallow freezer-proof lidded airtight container

INGREDIENTS
200g (7oz) vanilla sugar

400g (14oz) good-quality dark chocolate, 70% cocoa, chopped

2 tbsp honey

pinch of sea salt

1 Prepare the ice-cream maker as per the instructions. Heat the sugar and 700ml (1⅛ pints) water in a saucepan over a low heat, stirring occasionally, until the sugar dissolves. Increase the heat to medium and simmer for a further 5 minutes. Remove from the heat.

2 Start adding the chocolate to the pan, a little at a time. Whisk the mixture vigorously after each addition, to incorporate the chocolate into the syrup. Repeat until all the chocolate has been added.

3 Add the honey and salt to the mixture, and whisk to combine. Pour the syrup into a large heatproof bowl. Leave to cool completely, then chill until cold.

4 Pour the mixture into the ice-cream maker and churn for 30–40 minutes, as per the instructions. Once churned, transfer the sorbet to an airtight container and freeze for 3–4 hours, or preferably overnight. Serve in chilled bowls.

TIP If you can't find vanilla sugar, mix together 200g (7oz) caster sugar and ½ tsp good-quality vanilla extract.

Jesse Carr

CRICKETS OF THE NIGHT

This is inspired by the Grasshopper, a classic cocktail from 1920s New Orleans. I love the recipe, but until recently it was hard to find good-quality crème de cacao or crème de menthe. Using these liqueurs with intense absinthe and chocolate creates a more complex and interesting drink.

SERVES 1

WHAT YOU NEED

TIME
5 mins, plus freezing

SPECIAL EQUIPMENT
coupe glass

cocktail shaker

tea strainer

INGREDIENTS
30ml (1fl oz) crème de cacao

20ml (¾ fl oz) crème de menthe

10ml (¼ fl oz) absinthe

30ml (1fl oz) double cream

15ml (½ fl oz) VSOP Cognac

small handful of fresh mint, plus extra to garnish

ice cubes

good-quality dark chocolate shavings, 60% cocoa

1 About 5 minutes before making the cocktail, place the glass in the freezer.

2 Remove the glass from the freezer. Pour the liquid ingredients into the shaker. Add the mint, then fill the shaker with ice cubes.

3 Place the lid on the shaker, and shake hard for about 20 seconds, until you hear the ice crushing.

4 Place a tea strainer over the glass. Double-strain the cocktail by pouring it through the shaker's integral shaker and then through the tea strainer into the glass.

5 Serve immediately, topped with dark chocolate shavings and a sprig of mint.

GLOSSARY

BEAN-TO-BAR CHOCOLATE
Chocolate made directly from cocoa beans by one company, rather than several.

BLENDED CHOCOLATE
Chocolate made with beans of more than one variety or origin.

CHOCOLATE MAKER
A person or company who makes chocolate products directly from cocoa beans.

CHOCOLATIER
A person who makes bars, truffles, filled chocolates, and other chocolate confections from pre-made chocolate.

COCOA BUTTER
A naturally occurring fat found inside cocoa beans. Cocoa butter is often added to chocolate to make it smoother and easier to work with.

COCOA CAKE
The solid cocoa mass left behind after cocoa butter is removed from pressed beans.

COCOA NIBS
Pieces of shelled cocoa bean, usually roasted.

COCOA SOLIDS
A term used on chocolate packaging to describe the percentage cocoa content, usually including both cocoa beans and cocoa butter.

CONCHING
The process of stirring liquid chocolate over a prolonged period of time, in order to develop the flavour of the chocolate.

COUVERTURE
Chocolate designed for use by chefs and chocolatiers, usually with a high cocoa butter content.

CRIOLLO
One of the main cacao varieties, Criollo is considered to produce some of the best-quality cocoa beans in the world.

DARK MILK CHOCOLATE
Chocolate made with milk solids and a higher cocoa content than traditional milk chocolate.

DUTCH-PROCESS COCOA POWDER
Cocoa powder which has been treated to reduce acidity, giving it a nutty flavour.

FILLED CHOCOLATES
Thin chocolate shells filled with ganache, praline, or other ingredients.

FORASTERO
The most widespread variety of cocoa bean, generally cultivated for mass-produced chocolate.

GANACHE
A mixture of chocolate, cream, and sometimes butter. Used in truffles, filled chocolates, and cakes.

LECITHIN
A natural emulsifier that helps bind the ingredients in chocolate together.

MELANGER
A grinding machine designed to grind and refine cocoa nibs into liquid chocolate.

ROLL REFINER
A machine with multiple rollers used to refine chocolate.

SEIZING
Causing chocolate to become a thick, lumpy mass, seizing is the result of moisture coming into contact with liquid chocolate.

SINGLE-ESTATE CHOCOLATE
Made with cocoa beans from one estate or plantation, single-estate chocolate bars are created to showcase the unique flavours of that region.

SINGLE-ORIGIN CHOCOLATE
Chocolate bars made with beans from one country of origin. *See also* Blended chocolate.

TEMPERING
The process of melting and cooling chocolate at precise temperatures, in order to achieve a glossy sheen and a sharp "snap" when the chocolate is broken.

THEOBROMA CACAO
The scientific name for the cacao tree, meaning "food-of-the-gods cacao".

THEOBROMINE
A chemical found in cocoa beans that has been found to release endorphins in the brain, increase heart rate, and relax blood vessels.

TRAMPING
A technique for drying cocoa beans: farm workers walk through the beans, turning them with their feet to ensure even drying.

TRUFFLES
Small balls of ganache that have been dipped and/or rolled in cocoa powder, nuts, or other ingredients.

TREE-TO-BAR CHOCOLATE
Chocolate created by makers who grow and harvest cacao, and process the beans into chocolate bars themselves.

TRINITARIO
A variety of cacao cross-bred from Criollo and Forastero; named after the island of Trinidad, where it originated.

WINNOWING
The process of removing the outer shells from cocoa beans, leaving the nibs behind.

A NOTE ON COCOA VS CACAO
The words "cocoa" and "cacao" are used almost interchangeably in the chocolate industry today to refer to the fruit of *Theobroma cacao*. (For a note on word origins, see p15.) For the sake of clarity, this book uses *cacao* when referring to the farms, plantations, trees, pods, and beans prior to fermentation, and *cocoa* thereafter.

INDEX

Page numbers in **bold** refer to recipes; page numbers in *italics* refer to illustrations.

Project Editor
Martha Burley

Project Art Editor
Vicky Read

Editor
Alice Kewellhampton

Pre-Production Producers
Tony Phipps and Catherine Williams

Producer
Olivia Jeffries

Jackets Team
Libby Brown and Harriet Yeomans

Creative Technical Support
Sonia Charbonnier and Tom Morse

Managing Art Editor
Christine Keilty

Managing Editor
Stephanie Farrow

Art Director
Maxine Pedliham

Publishing Director
Mary-Clare Jerram

Illustrations Vicky Read
Photography William Reavell

First published in Great Britain in 2016 by
Dorling Kindersley Limited
80 Strand, London, WC2R 0RL

Copyright © 2016 Dorling Kindersley Limited
A Penguin Random House Company
2 4 6 8 10 9 7 5 3 1
001—285447—Sep/2016

Copyright © 2016 Dorling Kindersley Limited

A CIP catalogue record for this book is
available from the British Library.
ISBN 978-0-2412-2943-9

Printed and bound in China

A WORLD OF IDEAS:
SEE ALL THERE IS TO KNOW
www.dk.com

ABOUT THE AUTHOR

Dom Ramsey is a UK-based chocolate expert, bean-to-bar chocolate maker, and the founder and editor of *Chocablog*, the world's longest-running blog about chocolate. A regular judge for international chocolate competitions, Dom founded the award-winning chocolate company Damson Chocolate, after experiments in his own kitchen.

ACKNOWLEDGMENTS

Dom Ramsey would like to thank:
Margaux Benitah, Nat Bletter, Susana Cárdenas, Bob and Pam Cooper, Tim Davies, Mireille Discher, Lee Donovan, Jennifer Earle, Peter Galbavy, Laurent Gerbaud, Simon and Amy Hewison, Spencer Hyman, Kate Johns, Hazel Lee, Harmony Marsh, Samuel Maruta, Kim Russell, and Angus Thirlwell.

DK would like to thank:
Sara Robin for photography styling and art direction, Jane Lawrie for food styling, Linda Berlin for prop styling, Susannah Ireland for additional photography, Philippa Nash for design assistance, Amy Slack for editorial assistance, Steve Crozier for retouching images, Corinne Masciocchi for proofreading, and Vanessa Bird for indexing.

PICTURE CREDITS

The publisher would like to thank the following for their kind permission to reproduce their photographs.

(Key: a-above; b-below/bottom; c-centre; f-far; l-left; r-right; t-top)

10 Dorling Kindersley: Gary Ombler/Royal Botanic Gardens, Kew (bl). **21 Library of Congress**, Washington, D.C: (tr). **27 Dom Ramsey**: (cr). **32 Dom Ramsey**: (crb) **33 Dom Ramsey**: (tc,br). **51 Dorling Kindersley**: Gary Ombler / L'Artisan du Chocolat (cr). **51 Dorling Kindersley**: Gary Ombler /L'Artisan du Chocolat (br). **60 Bertil Åkesson**: (crb). **64 Dom Ramsey**: (br). **65 Dom Ramsey**: (t,b,cr). **86 Dom Ramsey**: (br). **87 Dom Ramsey**: (tl,ca,b). **116 Laurent Gerbaud**: (br). **117 Laurent Gerbaud**: (cra,b). **Dom Ramsey**: (tl). **132 Jason Economides**: (br). **133 The International Chocolate Awards**: Giovanna Gori (b). **Dom Ramsey**: (tl).

All other images © Dorling Kindersley
For further information see: www.dkimages.com

A NOTE ON THE MAPS
Cacao pod icons show the location of notable cacao-growing plantations on the maps on pp56–95. Yellow shading indicates cacao-growing over a larger area – either within political boundaries or over approximate climate-driven geographical areas.